SQUADRONS!

No. 61

THE BELGIAN FIGHTER SQUADRONS
- NOS 349 & 350 SQUADRONS -

PHIL H. LISTEMANN

ISBN: 978-2-494471-06-1

Copyright

© 2023 Philedition - Phil Listemann

Colour profiles: Gaetan Marie/Bravo Bravo Aviation

Special thanks to André Bar for his contribution

GLOSSARY OF TERMS

PERSONEL :
(AUS)/RAF: Australian serving in the RAF
(BEL)/RAF: Belgian serving in the RAF
(CAN)/RAF: Canadian serving in the RAF
(CZ)/RAF: Czechoslovak serving in the RAF
(NFL)/RAF: Newfoundlander serving in the RAF
(NL)/RAF: Dutch serving in the RAF
(NZ)/RAF: New Zealander serving in the RAF
(POL)/RAF: Pole serving in the RAF
(RHO)/RAF: Rhodesian serving in the RAF
(SA)/RAF: South African serving in the RAF
(US)/RAF - RCAF : American serving in the RAF or RCAF

RANKS
G/C : Group Captain
W/C : Wing Commander
S/L : Squadron Leader
F/L : Flight Lieutenant
F/O : Flying Officer
P/O : Pilot Officer
W/O : Warrant Officer
F/Sgt : Flight Sergeant
Sgt : Sergeant
Cpl : Corporal
LAC : Leading Aircraftman

OTHER
ATA: Air Transport Auxiliary
CO : Commander
DFC : Distinguished Flying Cross
DFM : Distinguished Flying Medal
DSO : Distinguished Service Order
Eva. : Evaded
ORB : Operational Record Book
OTU : Operational Training Unit
PoW : Prisoner of War
PAF: Polish Air Force
RAF : Royal Air Force
RAAF : Royal Australian Air Force
RCAF : Royal Canadian Air Force
RNZAF : Royal New Zealand Air Force
SAAF : South African Air Force
s/d: Shot down
Sqn : Squadron
† : Killed

CODENAMES - OFFENSIVE OPERATIONS - FIGHTER COMMAND

CIRCUS:
Bombers heavily escorted by fighters, the purpose being to bring enemy fighters into combat.

RAMROD:
Bombers escorted by fighters, the primary aim being to destroy a target.

RANGER:
Large formation freelance intrusion over enemy territory with aim of wearing down enemy figthers.

RHUBARD:
Freelance fighter sortie against targets of opportunity.

ROADSTEAD:
Dive bombing and low level attacks on enemy ships at sea or in harbour

RODEO:
A fighter sweep without bombers.

SWEEP:
An offensive flight by fighters designed to draw up and clear the enemy from the sky.

The Belgians in the RAF

Belgium entered the war in May 1940 when they were invaded by Germany. Belgian resistance ended after eighteen days. By late May 1940, the Belgians had 180 pilots and ground crew in Britain who had escaped from Belgium or France. They wanted them gathered into a Belgian unit, like the Dutch did the first early in June later followed by other nations, but that request was initially denied by the British because a large injection of RAF technical personnel would have been required to make the units operational. The Belgians were quickly re-trained and sent individually to various RAF combat units. About thirty of them participated in the Battle of Britain. This arrangement remained until the middle of 1941 when it was accepted that the Belgians could have their own units. It started slowly, however, with the formation of one flight into No. 131 (County of Kent) Squadron at the end of June 1941. This flight would serve as the nucleus for No. 350 (Belgian) Squadron at the end of the year. By that time the number of Belgians was enough to man a squadron without the support of RAF technical personnel. This time taken to form the squadron can be explained by the fact that the Belgians were almost entirely dependent on escapees from Europe, rather than volunteers from elsewhere, to build up their own force. However, they also had another asset to offer the British, their huge African colony, the Belgian Congo. Early in 1942, the Belgian authorities were extremely anxious about the vulnerability of the colony. To reinforce its defences, it was decided to raise two squadrons, one patrol unit with long-range aircraft to provide protection to the convoys, and one fighter squadron, although the need for the latter unit in the colony was less pressing. For the British, however, the threat was not that big, but it was finally agreed material would be provided to form a new fighter squadron, No. 349, with available Belgian personnel and British technical bods, the latter only temporarily. After much discussion among the politicians, 349 would, in the end, be based in West Africa, where the British needed a fighter presence that could be deployed to North Africa if required, and not in the Congo. Numbers 349 and 350 Squadrons were the only Belgian fighter units in the RAF during WW2.

That was the first step for a formation of a Belgian fighter squadron...during the autumn of 1941, a couple of Belgian pilots posing in front of a Spitfire of No. 131 Squadron in which a Belgian flight had been formed. The Belgian pilots on this photograph are:
In front of the wing L-R, two British officers, P/O G. Deltour, P/O E. Plas (†28.03.43 with 610 Sqn), F/L H. Gonay (†14.06.44 as OC 263 Sqn), P/O R. de Wever, P/O A. Plisnier, P/O D. Guillaume, P/O A. Boussa. Guillaume and Boussa would later take command of 350 Sqn.
(André Bar)

Victories - confirmed or probable claims: 57,0 + 6 o V 16

First operational sortie:
22.12.41

Last operational sortie:
05.05.45

Number of sorties: *ca.* 7,100

Total aircraft written-off: 72

Aircraft lost on operations: 57
Aircraft lost in accidents: 15

Squadron code letters:
MN

COMMANDING OFFICERS

S/L John M. THOMPSON	RAF No. 34183	RAF	12.11.41	20.03.42
S/L Désiré GUILLAUME	RAF No. 102953	(BEL)/RAF	20.03.42	19.12.42
S/L Adolphe BOUSSA	RAF No. 101465	(BEL)/RAF	19.12.42	06.01.44
S/L Léon PRÉVOT	RAF No. 84285	(BEL)/RAF	06.01.44	23.03.44
S/L Michel DONNET	RAF No. 102522	(BEL)/RAF	23.03.44	23.10.44
S/L Léopold COLLIGNON *(Inj.)*	RAF No. 116288	(BEL)/RAF	23.10.44	24.12.44
S/L Terence SPENCER *(Eva.)*	RAF No. 47269	RAF	04.01.45	26.02.45
S/L Frank F. WOOLLEY	RAF No. 105174	RAF	27.02.45	12.04.45
S/L Terence SPENCER *(PoW)*	RAF No. 47269	RAF	12.04.45	19.04.45
S/L Harold E. WALMSLEY	RAF No. 139425	RAF	23.04.45	19.08.45
S/L Rémi VAN LIERDE	RAF No. 106250	(BEL)/RAF	19.08.45	15.10.46

SQUADRON USAGE

As the first Belgian squadron formed in the RAF, 350 (Belgian) Squadron was raised from the Belgian flight of 131 (County of Kent) Squadron on 12 November 1941. The flight served as the nucleus of the squadron, but other Belgian personnel spread around various units were intended to join. The squadron was based at Valley on the Irish Sea. As 131 was already equipped with Spitfire Mk.IIs, it was logical that it would continue to work up on this mark. Command was given to S/L J.M. Thompson, a Battle of Britain veteran, who was commanding 131 Squadron at the time. Command of the ex-131's Belgian Flight was given to F/L H.A.C. Gonay, a Belgian and the second flight leader position went to F/L J. Carlier, also a Belgian and a new arrival from 135 Squadron. At first, 350 had no aircraft. The first arrived on the 25th, P7613, P8020 and P8652 coming from 610 Squadron. The previous day a Belgian pilot, Sgt A.Claesen, was seriously injured, and the aircraft wrecked, in a crash while attached to 3 Delivery Flight to deliver the Spitfires to 350. Three days later, it was turn of 74 Squadron to hand over aircraft with P7826, P7976, P8702 joining the fleet. At the end of November, the squadron was still forming, its 116 personnel including just 38 Belgians. The majority of the ground personnel was provided by the RAF, the British representing 75% of the total. In December, things were accelerated and more aircraft were taken on charge, coming mainly from 74 Squadron, but also from the MUs: P7297/A, P7376/X, P7378, P7509/M, P8033, P8040/H, P8091, P8144/J, P8146/E, P8149/G, P8174/S, P8200/T and P8377/C. Training commenced in early December and continued throughout the month without incident. As most of the pilots were already trained on the Spitfire, the work-up was rapid and, on 22 December, the squadron carried out its first operational sorties, a convoy patrol performed by A Flight. A Flight was the only one to be truly operational and it would be called to scramble a couple of times before the end of the month, but with no incidents to report upon return. In January 1942, both flights were operational and more than eighty sorties were flown, mainly convoy patrols. On 8 January, a mid-air collision occurred when, during formation practice, a Lysander of 6 AACU collided with the Spitfire flown by F/L Carlier. The Lysander crashed, killing its Polish pilot, but Carlier managed to return home where he force-landed his

Spitfire IIA P7297/MN-A was the regular mount of S/L J.M. Thompson. Note the Belgian flag painted under the cockpit, a practice that would soon be discontinued. Sometimes reported as a Mk V by the autumn 1941, it seems that it was still a Mk II when it was issued to 350 owing to the monthly technical reports and various other documents (logbooks or pilot's recollections).

damaged Spitfire. He was seriously injured and sent away for recovery. A logical change of command in B Flight took place, and P/O D.A. Guillaume arrived from 615 Squadron on the 17th to fill the B Flight commander position. In mid-February, the squadron was ordered to move east, to Atcham, south of Liverpool, giving up its convoy patrols at the same time. At the end of the month, 350 participated in Exercise 'Wrekin' and carried out reconnaissance sorties and ground attacks. This exercise was appreciated as it provided the opportunity to practice such roles. During the month, transition to the Spitfire Mk.V began and, by March, the last Spitfire IIs were withdrawn, the squadron moving to Warmwell in April to begin operations over the Continent. In all, 350 flew 164 sorties on the Spitfire II.

That month, Spitfires W3525/V, W3626/S, W3646/V, W3796, AA843, AA915/E, AA933/B, AA934, AA978/L and AB173/O were taken on hand and, soon after, a move from Valley to Atcham took place. The ferry flight to the new base was marred by a collision on landing at the new station of two Spitfires flown by F/Sgt H. Limet and P/O G. Seydel. This incident sealed the fate of Spitfire W3525 after only ten days with the squadron! The unit was commanded by S/L J.M. Thompson, a Battle of Britain veteran, but he relinquished command on 20 March to Belgian D. Guillaume, one of the two flight commanders. While the squadron was operational, its location, Atcham, south of Liverpool, was far from the front. Training occupied most of the pilots' time in March as the complement of Spitfire Mk.Vs was reached. However, on 29 March, Red section (Pilot Officers A. Plisnier and F. Vernosoen) was ordered to patrol base at 25,000 feet between 18.57 and 19.32. This was the first operational scramble since arrival at Atcham, but also the first sorties for the squadron's new Spitfires. The stay at Atcham was short as the Belgians soon received orders to move south to Debden, north of London, an airfield under 11 Group authority. This Group was the main organisation facing the Luftwaffe on the other side of the Channel. Before taking up residence at Debden, the squadron had to go to Warmwell to undertake a cannon-firing course between 6 and 15 April. While sixteen Spitfire Mk.Vs arrived at Warmwell, only fifteen left. On 12 April Sgt L. Hansez glided in too low over the trees and the engine did not pick up quickly enough when he applied power. Hansez escaped major injury, but the Spitfire was a write-off. The following few days were dedicated to administration and training. The first op with 11 Group took place on 25 April 1942 with the squadron engaged in convoy patrols all day. This tasking was repeated over the next two days, but nothing was reported. The first offensive operation over the Continent was carried out on the 28th with an escort of a flight of bombers. Only eleven Spitfires took off as F/L A. Boussa had a taxiing accident. The rest of the formation made the rendezvous with the Wing over Martlesham at 5000 feet before climbing to 22,000 feet and heading towards the French coast until opposite Mardyck. The squadron then left the Wing and flew along the French coast between Calais and Wissant to patrol the Strait of Dover as rear cover for returning bombers and fighters. On return, owing to oil trouble, P/O E. Plas had to land at Hawkinge as the rest of the squadron returned to Debden. The following day, in company with Nos. 111 and 71 (Eagle) Squadrons, 350 was airborne again to escort bombers. Nothing was reported if we ignore the fact that two Spitfires tipped on their noses, one while taxiing to take off (Sgt G. Livyns) and one on return (P/O R. Schrobiltgen). On the last day of April, the squadron was airborne for a Rodeo with Nos. 65 and 111 Squadrons, flying middle cover at 19,000 feet while 65 went to 18,000 feet and 111 was at 20,000 feet. The formation swept behind Ambleteuse, Marquise and Guines, then out between Calais and Gravelines before making a right turn to be over Dunkirk soon after. They saw enemy aircraft behind and to the right at least three miles away and a dogfight involving some

'Tommy' Thompson joined the RAF in 1934 and was posted to No. 29 Squadron in the following year. At the outbreak of war, he was a flight commander with No. 151 Squadron. He left that posting to take command of No. 111 squadron in January 1940. Flying Hurricanes, he opened his score in May 1940 when he claimed a Bf110 destroyed, another unconfirmed on the 18th and a He111 unconfirmed the following day. He was, however, shot down and crash-landed in a field before being evacuated by boat to England. He returned to operations before the end of the month and made further claims over Dunkirk. He then participated in the Battle of Britain and more claims led to the award of a DFC in September 1940. He was rested from October. He returned to operations in June 1941 to take command of the newly formed No. 131 (County of Kent) Squadron. This squadron had a Belgian flight that transitioned into a full squadron in November when it became No. 350 (Belgian) Squadron. Thompson was selected to lead this unit, the first Belgian fighter squadron in the RAF, and held this position until March 1942. At the end of July 1942, he was sent to Malta and appointed temporary WingCo Flying of the Takali Wing, then the Hal Far Wing between August 1942 and December 1942 and, subsequently until June 1943, the Luqa Wing. That gave Thompson the distinction of commanding all of Malta's Spitfire Wings over a period of ten months and also gave him the opportunity to make his last claims. His total was eight confirmed victories, five unconfirmed or probable (one shared) and seven aircraft damaged. A Bar to his DFC was awarded in December 1942 and was followed by a DSO in May 1943. He took a final operational posting in November 1943 when he led No. 338 Wing in French North Africa for a few months. He remained in the RAF after the war and held the rank of Air Commodore when he retired in September 1966.

Supermarine Spitfire Mk.IIA P7297
No. 350 (Belgian) Squadron
Squadron Leader J.M. Thompson
Valley (UK), December 1941

'Guilly' Guillaume, born in 1901, was rather old for a fighter pilot when the war broke out. He had joined the Belgian army in 1918, transferred to the Air Component in 1921 and became a fighter pilot two years later. In 1940 he was a Major, in a non-flying posting, leading the Air Firing School but, soon after the French armistice, he decided to flee to the UK. After brief training he joined No. 131 (County of Kent) Squadron, where a Belgian flight had been formed, at the end of August 1941 but left it soon after in October to serve with No. 79 Squadron and then No.615 (County of Surrey) Squadron. In January 1942 he was posted to the newly formed No. 350 (Belgian) Squadron as B Flight commander. Two months later he became the first Belgian OC of the squadron. He relinquished his command in December to take charge of RAF Hornchurch. He had received a DFC the previous October. He ended the war as a Group Captain and Inspector of the Belgian Air Force in Great Britain.

Supermarine Spitfire Mk.VB BM381
No. 350 (Belgian) Squadron
Squadron Leader D. Guillaume
Debden (UK), June 1942

twenty aircraft taking place. The Belgians were not engaged, but one Spitfire was damaged by flak (P/O G. Deltour) during the flight. He managed to return home, but the aircraft was eventually written off.

On 1 May, 350 flew close escort with the Wing for six Bostons targeting Saint-Omer. Intense flak was experienced over the target and Fw190s were about, but kept their distance. However, F/L Y. du Monceau de Bergendael opened fire at 600 yards without result. The squadron participated in two Rodeos and three Circuses over the next few days, but they were uneventful even though the first real, albeit inconclusive, combat with the Luftwaffe took place on the 6th off Boulogne. However, on the 9th, 350 scored for the first time when F/L Y. du Monceau de Bergendael claimed a Fw190 damaged while escorting bombers to the Hazebrouck marshalling yards during the morning. In the afternoon, the unit was sent with No. 65 Squadron to act as high cover for an attack on Bruges. After having crossed the Belgian coast, about a dozen enemy fighters appeared and combat was engaged. Sergeant J. Ester was able to get into a good position and fired, from 300 yards, at a Bf109 that was on the tail of the Spitfire flown by Sgt J. Blairon, with both cannon and machine guns. While Ester missed, his quarry did not. Blairon tried to reach the English coast, but jumped from less than 1000 feet into the Channel. An ASR mission was launched and was on the spot in a very short time to pick Blairon up, but he sadly died later that night. The squadron was released, either for training or for bad weather, and did not return to action until the 18th when it took part in an uneventful Rodeo with the Wing. *Circus* 175 took place the next day. With 71 (Eagle) Squadron, 350 acted as rear support for six Hurribombers attacking Saint-Omer. After the usual rendezvous, the Wing orbited a spot five miles off Cap Gris-Nez. At least thirty Fw190s were seen, alongside a few Bf109s, and both F/L Y. du Monceau de Bergendael and Sgt J.Ester went on the offensive. Both claimed a Fw190 as damaged. While crossing the French coast, Ester lost his numbers 1 and 2, so he began to weave. A Fw190 dived from behind and out of the sun, but Ester saw it in time and turned away, then reversed his turn and fired a short burst without visible results. He carried on weaving and saw a Bf109 ahead, climbing and turning towards him. He fired at it and saw a piece fly off from beneath its propeller. Almost immediately, he noticed a stream of glycol coming from its engine. Sergeant Ester claimed it as damaged, but as P/O R. Schrobiltgen (his No.2) reported seeing this Bf109 falling vertically with black smoke pouring from the engine, the claim was converted to a probable kill. Ester's adventure was not yet over. On the way back, about ten miles from the English coast, he noticed his aircraft's exhaust pipes becoming red hot. This was not a good sign and Ester decided to bale out while he was still at a good altitude (4000 feet). Being so close to the English coast made for an easy recovery and he was soon back with the squadron. The 20th was spent flying convoy patrols from Martlesham and, on the 21st, F/L A. Boussa and P/O G. Seydal carried out a Rhubarb attacking military objectives on the Nieuport - Dixmude -Thourout -Bruges - Blankenbergh route. No flying was performed on the 22nd. On the 23rd, the squadron was airborne for a Rodeo with the Debden Wing. Heading to Saint-Omer, the formation was heavily engaged, especially 350. The combat was fierce, at the end of which P/O A. Plisnier claimed one Fw190 destroyed and another damaged, while F/L A. Boussa and P/O R. Laumans each damaged a Fw190. These victories had a cost, however, with Pilot Officers L. Peeters and E. Winterbeek both posted missing. Peeters was later declared a PoW, but no trace of Winterbeeck was ever found. Until the end of the month, 350 was only airborne twice, on the 25th and 29th, for sweeps that proved uneventful.

One of the first Spitfire Mk.Vs taken on charge by 350 Sqn in February 1942 was BL540, which received the codes MN-Y. It was the mount of F/L du Monceau de Bergendael during the spring of 1942. The letter 'Y' was probably chosen as his first name was Yvan. *(André Bar)*

The squadron began June in the worst possible manner when three pilots were posted missing during a Wing escort of eight Hurribombers in the early afternoon. The Belgians were engaged by about twenty Fw190s while flying at 23,000 feet. Wing Commander J.A.G. Gordon, the Debden wing leader, was flying with 350. The Germans were able to split the Belgian formation with Blue section losing two pilots, Sgt J. Hansez and F/Sgt G. Livyns, while P/O R. Laumans of White section was also missing. Worse still, W/C Gordon was shot down and killed. Only P/O R. Laumans can be considered lucky as he survived to become a PoW. Not even the claim made by F/L Y. du Monceau de Bergendael, a Fw190 destroyed, could balance these losses. Despite this severe blow, 350 continued on operations, but suffered another loss on the 4th, P/O R. Schrobiltgen, while on a Rodeo, southwest of Cap Gris-Nez. He was seen to roll over slowly at 20,000 feet and enter a gentle dive. His wingman followed him down, to see when he pulled up, but lost him in cloud. Possibly a victim of hypoxia, Schrobilten was never seen again. This bad run of luck seemed to have come to an end as, during the following days, no further loss was reported while the squadron carried out Circuses, Rodeos, Rhubarbs and convoy patrols. Sadly, the Belgians suffered one more loss when Sgt M. Raes crashed on return from a convoy patrol on 13 June. He had lost his number one and was consequently given a vector to return home, but it seems that he flew too low and hit balloon cables near Norwich. While June had started badly, it finished on a high. On 29 June, 350 participated in Circus 195 to escort twelve Bostons to Hazebrouck. The squadron was tasked to fly at 16,000/17,000 feet. The target was reached without incident, but, on the return journey, the formation was attacked by Fw190s. They got P/O R. de Weaver who was last seen breaking away and diving steeply after having been on the tail of one of the Fw190s. It was later learned that he survived and was captured by the Germans. This time, however, this loss was balanced by the claim of two Fw190s destroyed, both made by P/O H. Picard. He went after a formation of Fw190s and initially closed in and shot at one of them from about 150 yards with a three or four second cannon burst. He saw the whole formation turn to the right at a moderate rate so he fired one or two deflection bursts before he suddenly saw a stream of brown smoke behind the last aircraft as it entered a dive. He could not see what happened next as he was attacked by other Fw190s. He performed some barrel rolls and shot at one of the Fw190s before he ran out of cannon shells. After this attack he saw a yellow splash in the sea below. He turned for home, but saw one of his squadron mates being attacked by a Fw190. He warned him on the R/T and turned left, but was soon attacked by another two Fw190s from behind and above. One of them was close so he pulled back on the control column until he almost stalled and turned over on his back. As the attacking Fw190 passed in front of him, about thirty to fifty yards away, he fired a deflection shot with his machine guns. He lost sight of the aircraft for a few seconds before seeing a green splash from an aircraft diving into the sea.

The number of sorties continued to increase in July, increasing from about 210 in June to 270, despite a total lack of activity during the first week of the month. This can be partially explained as 350 was deployed to Gravesend for six days, between the 1st and the 6th, where nothing really happened and no operations were carried out. Returning to Martlesham on the 7th, the squadron resumed operations the next day with convoy patrols throughout the day and an unsuccessful scramble by two aircraft. This activity was

In June 1942 F/L du Monceau de Bergendael changed his mount and began to fly EN794/MN-X. Note the swastikas painted under the cockpit and the irregular underwing roundels. These were caused by the introduction of a new roundel style in May 1942. The aircraft already in service had their existing roundels painted over as an immediate measure to obey the new regulation, but were soon painted the size described in the regulations. *(André Bar)*

Four Belgian pilots posing on four different 'Presentation' aircraft funded by the Belgian Congo Fund. Top left, P/O H. Picard on 'Luvungi' (EN796/MN-D). Top right, P/O A. Van der Haute on 'Kato'. Bottom left, P/O H. Smets on 'Popelin'. While the two first show a connection to places in the Belgian Colony, the latter was named after Marie Popelin, a lawyer and early leader of the feminist movement in Belgium. Bottom right, P/O M. Charlier on 'Stanley' (AB912/MN-W). The other 'Presentation' aircraft in this batch were 'Katanga', 'Albertville', 'Usoke', 'Elisabethville', 'Yaoundé', 'Lulanguru', 'Gambier', 'Hanssens', 'Crespel', 'Saisi', 'Leopoldville' and 'Baron Jacques'. Henri Picard was under training as a pilot when Belgium was invaded in May 1940 and he was evacuated to Britain with the school. He was shot down on 27 August while flying with 350 and taken prisoner. He would become one of the fifty men of the Great Escape to be recaptured and executed on 25 March 1944. Van der Haute was injured on 10 May 1940 by bomb splinters and spent the rest of the campaign in a hospital before escaping from Belgium and reaching Britain in June 1941. He survived the war. 'Le Flets' Smets was, like Picard, under training and travelled to England in the summer of 1940. He survived the war as a PoW when he was shot down in January 1945 while serving with 350 for another tour. Martin Charlier was the unit's oldest Belgian pilot as he was forty years old when Belgium was overrun. He was leading the only Belgian Hurricane unit at the time, but was wounded during a bombing raid of the aerodrome on 10 May. He made various attempts to evade to England before finding success and finally reached Britain in January 1942. He was quickly re-trained and joined 350 in July 1942 before being killed in action less than two months later. *(André Bar)*

A line-up of 350 Squadron's Spitfire Vs in June 1942 at Debden when the aircraft were given names in honour of the Belgian Congo Fighter Fund. In the forefront is Spitfire AR373/MN-M. Note the absence of a visible serial, a common practice in 1942, and the oversized underwing roundel as painted on EN794/MN-X on the previous page. *(André Bar)*

repeated until the squadron moved to Kenley on the 17th to become part of the Wing there. It resumed offensive operations two days later. On the 20th, Sgt R. Alexandre lost touch with the formation and flew inland over France. Two Bf109s engaged him after diving from the cloud. He fired at one, using five rings of deflection at 50 yards, when 100 feet off the ground. The other Bf109 attacked him and Alexandre broke off combat after he had fired a two second burst. Sergeant Alexandre saw no strikes and no claim was made on his return. On the 24th, as the weather became unsuitable for major operations, various Rhubarbs were flown. A section made up of Sergeants J. Rigole and F. Boute was the luckiest in finding barges to strafe on the Bray-Furnes canal near the France-Belgium border. All were hit and explosions recorded. Another section, consisting of Pilot Officers F. Vernsoen and H. Marchal, found a locomotive that they left enveloped in steam and flames. The next few days were quiet and few sorties were carried out, with none being over the Continent until the 28th when an incident free Rodeo was flown over Tricqueville aerodrome in company with the wing leader. Two days later, 350 participated in another major operation with the Wing, an escort for six Bostons attacking Abbeville, just before midday. In the evening, a second operation, a Ramrod, was carried out. The Wing orbited Saint-Omer where it was engaged by Bf109s and several separate combats ensued. Flight Lieutenant Y. du Monceau de Bergendael once more distinguished himself by claiming one Bf109 as probably destroyed and another as damaged, while Sgt J. Ester and P/O H. Marchal shared in the destruction of another. Marchal could not make it home and had to make a crash landing at Sandwich. The next day, 350 left for Tangmere to participate in a Ramrod mission with the Tangmere Wing. It was a busy day as the Belgians moved to Redhill that evening. At Redhill the Belgians were called upon more often and over 300 sorties were flown that month, the first time the squadron had reached that mark. However, after more than a month free of losses, the fortunes of war swung back. On 5 August, P/O G. Seydel was hit by flak while attacking railway targets between Diksmuide and Veurne. He managed, however, to make the journey back until, within fifteen miles east of Manston, he was obliged to bale out at 2000 feet. He was picked up soon after and returned safely to the squadron. Five days later an enemy aircraft was reported off Eastbourne and P/O X. Menu and Sgt J. Rigole took off into the very late evening sky. Ten/tenths cloud was reported at 400 feet with the cloud base at 100 feet. After ten minutes, Menu reported that it was dark and the section was given a vector back to Friston. However, it was found to be impossible to land at Friston so they were diverted to Tangmere. Rigole made it, but Menu did not and it was presumed that he had crashed in to the sea. On 13 August, the squadron was involved in several Rhubarbs, but P/O R. Dehasse fell victim to a take off accident and had to crash land near Lewes. He came through the ordeal okay, but the aircraft was a total write-off. Meanwhile the rest of the formation damaged four locomotives, one near Luneray, one five miles south of Dieppe, one five miles west of Yvelot, and the last one near Bolbec. Three days later, the squadron lost Sgt J. Ester during a similar kind of operation. While strafing a water tower, Ester collided with it and had to put down nearby but managed to evade capture and to return to the UK in April 1943. It was a dangerous game as P/O H. Picard from another section hit a high-tension cable, damaging a wing tip, but returned home. The Belgians participated in a Circus on the 17th and a Rodeo on the 18th. Both were uneventful. The big event of the month, not just for the Belgians, occurred the next day, the 19th, with Operation *Jubilee*, the Dieppe landings, well and truly underway. It was a really big day for all units engaged in this operation, including 350 which carried out 47 sorties over four ops (07.20, 10.00, 12.20 and 15.15). The Luftwaffe reacted swiftly in force and a fierce battle took place over the town. The first to score was Sgt L. Flohimont who damaged a Fw190, a claim followed soon after by another one, a Fw190 shot down in flames by F/L Y. du Monceau de Bergendael, while P/O H. Picard and E. Plas shared in the destruction of another. However, the Belgians lost one of their own, P/O H. Marchal but he was luckily picked up out of the sea and returned to the squadron. On the second op, 350 added two Fw190s destroyed (F/L A. Boussa and P/O F. Venesoen), a probable (Sgt R. Alexandre) and five damaged (Alexandre, Boussa, Sgt F. Boute, F/L Y. du Monceau de Bergendael and P/O G. Seydel). In this engagement, Boussa was wounded in a leg, but this did not prevent him from participating in the other ops of the day. He conducted a third flight, a patrol at 6000 feet to cover the withdrawal of ground forces. More claims were made. A Ju88 was shot down by Yellow section (Sgt J. Vanlerberghe, P/O H. Smets, P/O A. Plisnier and Sgt F. Boute). They saw the tail unit fall off and the aircraft was seen diving into the sea shortly after. The last sortie was to escort returning vessels, but the Luftwaffe was still active and more combats ensued. The Belgians made the best of an advantage over the German pilots, with only two Spitfires slightly damaged in return for one Fw190 claimed as destroyed by Plisnier, six claimed as damaged (two for Alexandre, and one each for Flohimont, Seydel, Venesoen and Plas). Sergeant Van Lerberghe also attacked a Do217 and damaged it. In addition to the intensive efforts made that day, the Belgians had further opportunities to score as they continued their regular ops over the Continent until the end of the month. On 27 August, the squadron took part in *Circus* 208 to escort twelve Bostons. The Luftwaffe tried to intercept and some combats developed north of Le Crotoy. Flight Lieutenant Y. du Monceau de Bergendael made another claim for a destroyed Fw190 while F/O E. Plas claimed another probably destroyed and one damaged, but at the cost of P/O H. Picard, who became a PoW, and P/O M. Charlier, who was killed. An uneventful Rodeo was performed the next day and the month ended quietly with some convoy patrols. The operational tempo reduced in September and the Belgians had to wait until the 6th to go over to the Continent again for an uneventful Circus escorting bombers to Boulogne. In the second week of September, the squadron was sent to an air-firing course at Martlesham, operational activity resuming on the 16th with some convoy patrols. On 21 September, Yellow section went to Friston to carry out an operational patrol. Late in the afternoon, P/O F. Venesoen and Sgt L. Heimes acted as a R/T link for a section of No. 611 Squadron looking for a Mustang that had ditched. The Belgians were called back, but the weather deteriorated. Sergeant Heimes tried to land at the now unserviceable Friston. He damaged his undercarriage so he took off again. At that moment, his instruments, other than the turn and bank, failed so he was ordered to evacuate the aircraft. He landed without a scratch. Venesoen did not fare any better. He was vectored to base, but was unable to locate the aerodrome because of low cloud and the dark sky. Flying low, he finally hit a tree on a hill near Godstone and crashed. Venesoen suffered abrasions to his head and face and smashed his knee cap. The remainder of the month was relatively quiet and operational activity

Another 'Presentation' Aircraft was named 'Stanley' after New York Herald newspaper correspondent Henry M. Stanley famous for his meeting at Ujiji on Lake Tanganyika in 1871 with the Scottish explorer Dr. David Livingstone. Here, too, no serial is visible, but the underwing roundels do obey the new RAF regulation of May 1942. *(André Bar)*

reduced to convoy patrols out of Southend on the Thames estuary from the 23rd. At Southend, the number of sorties increased, with more than 310 recorded in October, but as the weather is not the best during that time of year, operations over the Continent were limited to Circuses, Rodeos or sweeps flown on the 2nd, 9th, 11th, 12th and 25th (one recalled en route on the 17th). At that time the Belgians were working closely with the Australians of No. 453 Squadron. The rest of the sorties consisted of patrols and the occasional scramble. On the administrative side, S/L Guillaume was awarded the DFC. With winter approaching the weather had an impact on flying activity. Less than 150 sorties were flown in November and only about 130 were achieved in December. The number of shows over the Continent diminished in November, with two Ramrods (6th and 24th), one Circus (8th) and one Roadstead (24th). No major incidents were reported. On the other hand, however, some Rhubarbs were carried out on the 16th and 19th and in both cases the Belgians found luck. Indeed, during the first one, P/O F. Venesoen and F/O A. Plisnier encountered a venerable Ju52 flying at 400 feet as the formation was headed northwards to Saint-Aubin aerodrome. The first to attack was Venesoen with a head-on pass that resulted in hits. Plisnier followed up with a short burst, firing with slight deflection and observed three hits in the rear of the fuselage. It was the fatal shot for the transport aircraft as it crashed, turned over and burst into flames. The claim was shared by the two pilots. On the second Rhubarb, P/O A. Plisnier was flying with Sgt L. Harmel. They crossed the Belgian coast eight miles east of Knocke, skirting some bad weather. Then they followed the Bruges-Ghent railway line. Flying at about 400 feet, they saw a Bf110 flying at the same altitude and about to land at Ghent aerodrome. Plisnier was the first to attack with a head-on pass, firing first from 1000 yards, but with no results. Sergeant Harmel followed and attacked with a deflection shot from 150 yards, closing to twenty. Pieces were seen flying from the Bf110 around the left engine. Plisnier made another attack from astern and blew off the tailplane, causing the German aircraft to turn over. Upon hitting the ground, it disintegrated. Here, too, the claim was shared by both pilots. Nothing else of note happened until the squadron moved to Hornchuch on 8 December. The first major op from that station occurred on the 12th, a Circus, with the Belgians flying alongside 453 Squadron. The Belgians crossed the French coast at 27,000 feet when Fw190s appeared and were engaged over Saint-Omer. A series of dogfights ensued and the Belgians lost one of their own, F/O W. de Merode, while P/O A. Plisnier managed to return home with a seriously damaged aircraft. He filed a report for two Fw190s damaged during this action as did F/O L. Collignon and F/L Y. du Monceau de Bergendael. As for de Merode, he survived and evaded capture, returning to the UK in March 1943. One week later a major change occurred within the squadron as S/L Guillaume relinquished command to F/L A. Boussa, the A Flight commander. Boussa's position was taken over by P/O H. Smets. It was not Boussa who led the next operation the following day, however, as F/L Y. du Monceau de Bergendael led the Belgians on an uneventful Circus in the company of Nos. 122 (Bombay) and 453 (RAAF) Squadrons. The year ended with a squadron scramble that evolved into a base patrol.

The New Year started with a diversion operation to Abbeville with 122 Squadron. The squadron was led by the new Wing Commander Flying W/C A.M. Bentley. The op was uneventful as were the next major operations, all Circuses, on the 9th, 13th and

Sgt J. Wustefeld and P/O G. de Patoul in front of Spitfire EE766/MN-C during Exercise *Spartan* (note the distinctive white bands painted on the nose). Guy de Patoul was a former regular artillery officer who managed to escape to England in June 1940. He enlisted in the RAF in August and served one year with 610 Sqn before joining 350 Sqn in September 1942. He ended the war as a PoW on 24 April 1945 while completing a second tour of operations. Jacques Wusterfeld was also serving in the Belgian army when he was evacuated, but only enlisted in the RAF in September 1941. He joined 350 direct from training in December 1942. He survived the war. (André Bar)

Adolphe Boussa
RAF No. 101465

A pre-war regular officer with the Aéronautique Militaire, Boussa was in charge of a fighter unit flying the Fairey Fox in May 1940. During the Phoney War, he participated in the action which forced an Armstrong Whitworth Whitley to make a forced landing in Belgium on 9 September 1939. He led his unit to France and, in August 1940, returned to occupied Belgium, only to flee the country a week later. The journey was long; he only arrived in Britain in June 1941. Retrained as a fighter pilot in just a couple of weeks, he served in various front-line RAF squadrons before joining No. 350 (Belgian) Squadron in March 1942 as a flight commander. Boussa made his first claim on 23 May, an Fw190 probably destroyed over Calais. In December, he was given command of the squadron; it was in this position that he made his final claim, a Do217 destroyed on 6 April 1943. His score had reached two aircraft destroyed, one probable and one damaged. He left the squadron as CO in January 1944 and, being too old (39) to have his wish for another tour of operations granted, decided to join Special Service Duties (SOE). In April, he was dropped in to Occupied Europe where he formed camps for escaped Allied aircrew. It was only in August 1944 that he managed to cross into Allied territory. For his actions with the SOE, he received the Military Cross.

Supermarine Spitfire Mk.VB AD288
No. 350 (Belgian) Squadron
Squadron Leader A. Boussa
Acklington (UK), summer 1943

Supermarine Spitfire Mk.VB AR498
No. 350 (Belgian) Squadron
Squadron Leader A. Boussa
Digby (UK), autumn 1943

Spitfire MN-Z being prepared for another flight at its dispersal during the summer of 1943. This aircraft has clipped wings (as does the one visible behind it). *(André Bar)*

21st. The unit lost a pilot during the next Circus (22nd) when F/Sgt L. Frohimont was shot down and killed by Fw190s. That occurred just after the bombing of Saint-Omer aerodrome. The Belgians turned right and, when they were facing Mardyck, some Fw190s flying in loose pairs were seen at 3 o'clock. Sergeant R. Alexandre was one of the first to react and he made a turning climb to the right. Two Fw190s ahead of the others broke upwards in an unusual steep climb. One went over onto its back and dived toward the formation. Being 1000 feet above, Sgt Alexandre followed the Fw190 in his dive and easily kept up. Upon reaching the coast at Mardyck, the Fw190 pulled out at about 200 feet and made a steep turn to the left. Alexandre turned inside the Focke-Wulf, pulled up, throttled back and fired a one second burst with four to five rings of deflection. He lost sight of the 190 for a second before seeing it again as its left wing hit the sea. He claimed this Fw190 as destroyed, but he was not the only one to make a claim during the engagement. Pilot Officer A. Plisnier returned with a probably destroyed Fw190. The two other Circuses of the month (25th and 26th) were uneventful. In January, other operations of this nature were cancelled because of bad weather and were sometimes replaced by Rhubarbs. In all, the Belgians flew close to 190 sorties which wasn't that bad for a month when the forces of nature usually rule the roost. February remained quiet with about eighty sorties flown and these were mostly achieved over four major operations – *Rodeo* 169 on the 16th, *Circus* 269 the following day, and *Circus* 274 on the 26th, a tasking repeated twice that day for a total of 36 sorties. Between 1 and 12 March, 350 participated in Exercise *Spartan*. The Belgians returned to operations on the 13th with convoy patrols followed by two Rodeos with Nos. 453, 64 and 122 Squadrons. This was to be the last op from Hornchurch as the squadron moved to Fairlop, close to London, the next day, before moving again to Acklington, north of Newcastle, on the 24th. Acklington would be the squadron's home for the next ten weeks. It was not the best place to see action, but that was the point as 350 needed a rest after an intense summer. Operational activity consisted of patrols or scrambles and during the ten weeks less than sixty sorties were logged. However, one pilot was particularly lucky. On 6 April 1943, the CO took off for some local flying when he was diverted to intercept an enemy aircraft spotted in the area. Two sections of the squadron scrambled, but he was the first to make contact when he identified a Do217 flying at ground level. Without hesitation, S/L A. Boussa made a diving attack from 3/4 to head-on, slightly on the Dornier's left side. At about 1000 yards he opened fire with a short burst of cannons and machine guns to get the correct deflection. He then fired one long burst from about 800 yards until he had passed over the German bomber. During this burst he saw strikes on the sea all around the aircraft. The Do217 turned to the right, dived into the sea and sank immediately about

60 miles from the coast. On 8 June, 350 moved to Ouston, not very far from Acklington, where, of course, activity remained negligible. On 11 July, a dramatic accident occurred when F/O R. Van de Poel and Sgt M. Grawels, returning from a cross-country, collided in the air as they approached to land. Neither of them had time to evacuate their aircraft and they were killed in the subsequent crash. The Belgians returned to Acklington on 20 July. They stayed there until they moved south to Digby on 25 August. Until the end of the year, they were located at a variety of bases – West Malling (7-18 September), back to Digby, Hawkinge (1-13 October), Southend (13-31 October) and then back to Hawkinge again. Apart from training and practice, little operational flying was done with as few as eight sorties flown in August (six convoy patrols in three sections on the 12th and one scramble on the 17th). At West Malling, 350 participated in two Ramrods on the 8th, the first being an escort for bombers attacking Vitry-en-Artois. The op was carried out successfully without loss. The second one, escorting bombers to the Boulogne area, was also completed without loss. The next day was dedicated to shipping patrols, 34 flown for the whole day. This was to be the busiest day of the month as only ten more sorties were reported for the remainder of the month. October was no better with one Ramrod on the 2nd (No. 256) and another on the 8th (No. 264).

November could be considered as a re-start for the Belgians who flew more than 200 sorties during the month. They were heavily involved in close escorts of bombers, both RAF and USAAF. The Allies had begun to exert pressure on the Germans and many targets had to be neutralised as D-Day was approaching (not that the pilots knew this of course). When the Belgians were not occupied with escorting bombers, they carried out sweeps over the Continent as part of Rhubarb operations. It was during one such op that F/Sgt F. Boute and Sgt M. de Hepcée were posted missing on the 13th. The squadron continued on the same path into December even though bad weather had a negative impact on operational activity. On 20 December, the Belgians were airborne twice. While the first escort in the morning was flown without incident, things did not go so well for the second escort early in the afternoon. The op was to escort RAF Mitchells to Audinghen. On the way back, the squadron left the bombers over the sea and returned to France with another striking force. An unidentified aircraft was seen flying very fast at 25,000 feet in a north-west direction from Abbeville. The Belgians climbed to 17,000 feet, but could not intercept. The squadron re-crossed the French coast south of Hardelot and on the way out near Abbeville, F/Sgt L. Harmel turned back with engine trouble. Flight Lieutenant L. Collignon followed him down to 2000 feet near Doullens, but broke away on seeing tracer fire from the ground. While at 2000 feet, he saw and attacked a 'Noball' target north east of Abbeville, observing strikes on buildings. As far as F/Sgt Harmel was concerned, he was forced to make an emergency landing, but managed to evade capture, returning to the UK in February 1944. This 'temporary' loss was compensated for during a close escort mission for Mitchells to Purchevin the following day. The raid was executed without incident and 350 turned back and crossed the sea. The operations room reported twelve 'bandits' approaching from 3 o'clock. The section led by F/L Collignon was slightly separated from the rest of the formation and ordered to head towards the contact. Combat was soon engaged with Fw190s. Only F/O A. Herreman managed to get in to a good position and, in two short attacks on the same aircraft, was able to hit it. He last saw the Focke-Wulf roll on its back and go into the sea four miles off Le Touquet. This victory was followed one week later by another one during a Crossbow Rhubarb. The formation of five Spitfires, led by F/L A. Plisnier, crossed the French coast at sea level and met intense flak. They approached the target, German facilities at Gueschart, near Abbeville, at ground level, then climbed to 1000 feet. During the attack, the Belgians were surprised by Fw190s. Flying Officer A. Claesen was the first to be

The end of summer 1943 while on detachment at West Malling. From left to right, the pilots identified are Sgt A. Van Wersch, F/Sgt L. Harmel, Sgt R. Bladt, unknown (showing the back), unknown (showing the back), P/O J. Lavigne and unknown (from behind). Seated on the wing, Sgt G. de Jeagher, unknown and F/O L. Lelarge. Note the Belgian roundel painted under the exhaust. AD288 was S/L A. Boussa's mount during the summer 1943 before it was replaced by AR498. *(André Bar)*

Léon Prévot joined the Belgian *Aéronautique Militaire* as an NCO in May 1934. In 1939 he was serving as a flying instructor. He was commissioned in February 1940 and in May was serving with the flying school with which he fled to France, then French Morocco, and eventually arrived in Great Britain in August 1940. He joined the RAF upon his arrival. He was re-trained and posted to No. 235 Squadron to fly Blenheims. In December he left to instruct French-Belgians at Odiham. In August 1941, after a refresher course at No. 58 OTU on Spitfires, he was posted to No. 123 Squadron, but, soon afterwards, was posted to No. 64 Squadron as a flight commander. He was given command of No. 122 (Bombay) Squadron in May 1942 but was shot down over France on 30 July only to evade capture with the help of the French Resistance and return to England in mid-October. The next month he was awarded the DFC shortly after being posted to No. 65 Squadron. He only stayed there for two weeks as he was posted to No. 197 Squadron as its first OC flying Typhoons. He remained with 197 until June 1943 when he was posted out for a rest. Six months later he returned to operations by assuming command of No. 350 Squadron. In March 1944, promoted to wing commander, he left 350 and served in various HQ positions until the end of war. Serving with the Belgian Air Force post-war, he retired in January 1964.
(André Bar)

attacked, but managed to break off to the left, but F/Sgt G. Dancot received direct hits. He was seen crashing in flames. Flying Officer L. Siroux and P/O J. Lavigne were also attacked, but their reactions enabled them to engage. When F/O Siroux saw tracers around him, he immediately broke to the left at zero feet. At that moment one Fw190 came straight into his gunsight and he instinctively fired a two second burst starting with one ring deflection at 300 yards and finishing at 200 yards. However, he lost sight of the Fw190 when he was again fired upon and dived towards the ground. He saw two Fw190s firing and climbing as they came into his sight. He fired on the first one, but soon ran out of cannon ammunition. He then put his nose down so did not see the results, but after consulting his leader's report of an aircraft crashing, he made a claim for a confirmed destroyed Fw190. Unknown to the Belgian, this claim would be the last on the Spitfire V. On 30 December, the squadron re-equipped with the more potent Spitfire IX, the first example received on the 30th. That day 350 moved to Hornchurch where it took charge of the Spitfire Mk.IXs previously flown by No. 222 (Natal) Squadron. The pilots used the beginning of January 1944 to master their new mounts and carried out their first Spitfire IX sorties on the 6th with a Ranger of four aircraft, over occupied Belgium around midday, followed by another a bit later. The sector chosen was Renaix-Courtrai and Tournai. A short skirmish occurred between the first section and Fw190s, but the Germans were quick to leave the area, while the second section flew an uneventful sortie. The same day, S/L Boussa ended his tour of operations and was replaced by S/L L. Prevot. Over the next two days, 350 flew one sweep and two Ramrods (Nos. 431 and 440). Nothing else was flown until the 21st, but regular flying resumed from then until the end of the month. In all, eight

Four Belgian pilots posing in front of a Spitfire IX.
Left to right, F/L L. Collignon (flight CO at the time, he would later command 350 Sqn in the autumn of 1944 before being severely wounded in action in December 1944), Flying Officers J. Lavigne and P. Siroux (he was later posted to 349 Sqn), and P/O J. Wustefeld.
(André Bar)

Ramrods and two Rangers were flown during that period of time. All were uneventful until the Rangers were carried out. January 30 started badly when *Ramrod* 499 was cancelled due to bad weather. They were replaced by two Rangers (Nos. 7 and 8) in the afternoon. The first section, led by F/L L. Collignon, crossed the French coast near Nieuport and headed to Tournai where some barges were strafed near Saint-Omer. Not far from there, buildings were also strafed, as were gun posts near Calais, but, while doing so, F/O G. Duchesne, who was flying number two to Collignon, was shot down by flak. The aircraft crashed near Sainte-Marie-Kerke with Duchesne still on board. The second section, led by F/L R. Alexandre, didn't have any better luck as the formation was caught by flak heading to Saint-Pol-sur-Ternoise. Flying Officer J. Gérard was hit and obliged to leave the formation, heading home with a badly damaged Spitfire accompanied by P/O F. Verpoorten. While landing at Hawkinge, however, Gérard stalled, crashed and the Spitfire caught fire. Sadly, he did not survive. During the first week of February, 350 flew three uneventful Ramrods before it was sent on a ten-day Air Firing Course at Llanbedr. Returning to Hawkinge on the 20th, operations resumed on the 22nd with *Ramrod* 577. The squadron participated in six more Ramrods before the end of February. All were uneventful. In March, the unit continued its escort work, six being flown in the first week before a move to Scotland left the Spitfire IXs behind and the 350 returned to flying the Mk.V. During this first phase of the Mk.IX, 350 recorded about 330 sorties on the type. For their rest period, 350 moved to Peterhead in Scotland, north of Aberdeen, still under the command of S/L L. Prévot who had been in charge since January. As the Spitfire Mk.IX was not as desperately needed in this quiet area of the war, the Belgians reverted to the Spitfire Mk.V. In Scotland, operational activity was reduced to convoy patrols, but the bulk of flying activity consisted of training and practice. On 21 March, Sgt M. Morel experienced engine failure over the sea while practicing formation flying and ditched his aircraft. He was lucky to be picked up after just four minutes by a nearby fishing boat. Remaining much longer in the cold waters of Scotland at this time of the year could have been fatal. Three days later, S/L M. Donnet arrived to assume command from S/L L. Prévot. A few days later, 350 lost another Spitfire V when F/O G. Beckers experienced engine trouble, again while practicing formation flying, and had to bale out.

The stay in Scotland was short, however, as the squadron moved south on 26 April, heading to Friston, between Brighton and Hastings, in anticipation of the D-Day landings. The unit was not part of 2 TAF as it remained under 11 Group authority. The Belgians shared the aerodrome with the pilots of 501 Squadron. They recommenced ops with patrols during the first few days at Friston before participating in a close escort of 36 Bostons. However, the op started badly as two aircraft collided two minutes after take off. The Spitfire flown by F/O D. Scuvie went under the aircraft flown by F/O G. de Jaegher. The tail of Scuvie's Spitfire was sliced by de Jaegher's propeller and immediately entered a spin. Scuvie had no time to bale out as the Spitfire fell into the sea. Flying Officer de Jaegher's aircraft became uncontrollable and he had to ditch, fortunately without major injury. In May, the Belgians were

Just before D-Day, 350 saw some British pilots to be posted in to reinforce the squadron. Three of them are here posing, from left to right, F/Sgt P.A. Wilson, F/Sgt J. F. Woolley and F/L E.H.M. Patterson. Peter Wilson was killed soon after on 10 June and Joseph Woolley the following 8 July on a Spitfire Mk IX. Eric Patterson, born in Chili from British parentage was posted to 229 Sqn in July and was given command of this unit later in the year. He survived the war with a DFC.
(André Bar)

Michel Donnet

RAF No. 102522

'Mike' Donnet enlisted in the pre-war Belgian military forces to become a pilot. In May 1940, he was flying the Renard R.31, a Belgian co-operation aircraft, with the Army. He was made a PoW on 28 May and sent to Germany but was released in January 1941. He returned to Belgium but fled to Great Britain in July in an SV-4 biplane that had been hidden on the property of one of his friends. Upon arrival in England, he enlisted in the RAF, was re-trained and, in September, joined No. 64 Squadron. He opened his score on 30 March 1942 by claiming two Fw190s damaged. More successes followed and in September 1942 he became a flight commander and then, eventually, the OC in March 1943. The previous January, he had been awarded the DFC. His first tour ended in November and he made his last claim of the war, a Bf109 probably destroyed, on the 3rd to bring his total to three confirmed victories, two probables and six aircraft damaged. He returned to operations in March 1944 as OC of No. 350 (Belgian) Squadron and led the unit until October when he became the WingCo Flying of the Hornchurch Wing. He led the Mustang-equipped Bentwaters Wing in the same role from February 1945. Donnet, therefore, became one the very few Belgian pilots to fly Mustangs operationally during the war. He left the Wing in August and was discharged from the RAF in October 1946. Continuing his career in the new Belgian Air Force, he reached the rank of Lieutenant General and retired in 1975.

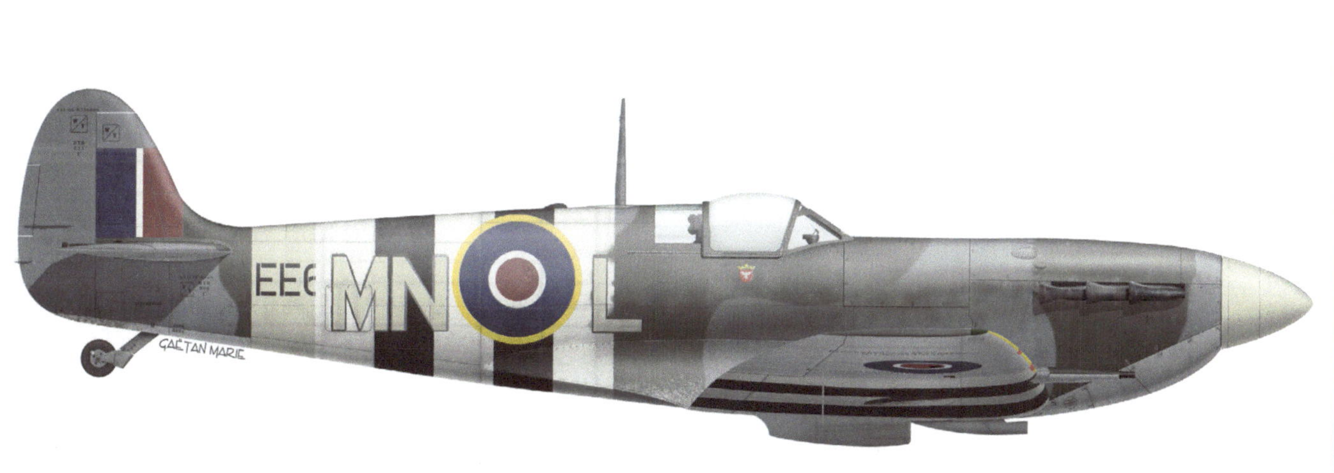

Supermarine Spitfire Mk.VC EE613
No. 350 (Belgian) Squadron
Squadron Leader M. Donnet
Friston (UK), June 1944

'Mike' Donnet in his Spitfire EE613 in June 1944. *(André Bar)*

intensively employed and 335 sorties were carried out. The squadron performed fifteen escorts, four sweeps and one mass Rhubarb operation. No losses were reported.

On the eve of the D-Day landings, 350 could count on 23 pilots, with S/L M. Donnet as CO and Flight Lieutenants R. Alexandre and A. Plisnier as the flight commanders. The first days of June were occupied with patrols and shipping reconnaissances. On D-Day, the Belgians were airborne at 04.35 to cover the landings. Over the Channel, F/L F. Venesoen had to bale out due to an internal glycol leak. His number 2, F/O L. Siroux, followed his leader and saw him evacuate his aircraft correctly and the chute open. He watched Venesoen land in the water and struggle to inflate his dinghy. Siroux guided three launches to the spot, but eventually no trace of the Belgian could be found. The rest of the formation landed at 06.35. At 09.35, Flying Officers R. Vanderveken and J. Wusterfeld took off on a base scramble and patrolled for one hour before returning to land, the Wing Co Flying, W/C D.E. Kingaby, flying with the Belgians. Soon after they had taken off, the second patrol of the day was flown, over the beaches at 3000 feet, but proved uneventful. A third patrol between 22.20 and 23.30 was achieved at the same altitude, but was also quiet. The workload was heavy for all squadrons involved in the invasion. Over the next few days, which were critical to the success of Operation *Overlord*, the Belgians carried out 118 sorties (except on the 9th as bad weather stopped play), but no real opposition was met. Danger remained ever present, however. On the 7th, the Spitfire of F/O R. Vanderveken was damaged by a 40mm shell, but he managed to return to base. The next day, the squadron, led by W/C D.E. Kingaby, was caught very late in the evening in very poor visibility and a cloud base of 300/400 feet. The aerodrome was accessible, but every pilot landed somewhere else, most at Deanland, but F/O A. Herreman did not make it. Soon after the other members of 350 had landed, two crashes were reported in the vicinity of Friston aerodrome. It was the CO who discovered the wreckage after two hours of searching. The Spitfire had crashed in the hills with the wreckage of a second aircraft, an American Maraudeur. It was believed that the two aircraft collided in cloud. Two days later, 350 lost another pilot, its A Flight CO, F/L R. Alexandre. While flying at 1800 feet over the beachhead area, he experienced engine failure and called a Mayday. The aircraft was seen to be out of control in a slight diving glide and swinging to the right and left. At 600/700 feet, the Spitfire went into a 45° dive and crashed into the sea. Flying Officer L. Lelarge circled for twenty minutes over the patch left by the aircraft, but could not see anything floating. Alexandre was posted missing. In the meantime, Blue section, consisting of F/L E. Paterson, F/O P. Wilson, P/O A. Van Wersch and F/Sgt J. Laloux, chased a Bf109 south of Caen. Paterson and Wilson were two British pilots who had recently arrived to reinforce the squadron. The chase was inconclusive as none of the pilots managed to get into range. However, Wilson, who was flying as Paterson's No. 2, disappeared and was posted missing. Over the following days various incidents continued to plague the squadron's activity even though none were to be fatal either for the pilot or aircraft. However, on 12 June, the squadron was close to accepting the loss of another pilot when F/O R. Muls was posted missing after he transmitted a message reporting a glycol leak. Fortunately, he was found safe the next day at Southampton after he had made a forced landing in France in Allied held territory. Things did not go so well for F/O L. Lelarge on the 14th, however. During a patrol he experienced engine trouble 15 miles off Saint-Aubin which forced him to bale out over the Channel. The squadron turned back immediately, but no trace of a parachute or dinghy was found. The worst was feared, but Lelarge was later declared safe after having been rescued by the Royal Navy. He returned to the squadron two days later. It was to be the last loss recorded by 350 while it flew the Spitfire V. The squadron continued to carry out patrols over the beachhead, but as the Allies were now advancing into Normandy, no opposition was really expected. However, this doesn't mean that nothing happened. On 27 June, F/L A. Plisnier fired at a Me410 five miles off Cherbourg, but the German aircraft disappeared into clouds and no claim was made. The next day the same pilot chased two Fw190s north of Caen with six Mustangs on their tails, but soon abandoned the chase. Finally, on 28 June, during a patrol led by the CO around the Le Havre area, eight Bf109s were sighted west of Cabourg flying south. The Germans disappeared before the Belgians could react. When the end of the month came, the sortie tally, 630, revealed just how busy the squadron had been. The last patrols from Friston were carried out on 1 July, then, after two days of bad weather, the squadron moved to Westhampnett where it exchanged the venerable Spitfire Vs for brand new Spitfire IXs, now the standard Spitfire variant employed by the RAF. During that day, the squadron flew 24 patrols over the beachhead. When the pilots of the final patrols landed at Westhampnett around 23.30, the end of a long association with the Spitfire V had arrived. Indeed, the next day, training was carried out on the new mount and, the day after, the first Spitfire IX ops were flown. At that time the last operational Spitfire Mk Vs on charge were W3305/A, W3521, W3759/N, W3768, W3828/R, W3970/D, AB380/X, AB848/W, AR429, BL631/B, BL755/H, BM583/T, EE613/L, EN800, EN957, EP253, EP664/Y, EP687/E. Some Spitfire Mk Vs were kept for training duties until the end of the summer 1944. Therefore, the Belgians and 350 Squadron had one of the longest operational periods with the Spitfire V in the RAF.

It was time to switch to a variant with more performance and 350 was notified early in July that it would re-equip with the Mk.IX again over the next few days (MH499/Y, MJ243/M, MJ338/D, MJ424, MJ521/R, MJ790, MJ890/X, MJ900/N, MK208/I, MK298/B, MK301, MK319, MK606/W, ML137/Z, ML294/E, PL288/L). Of course, no transition period was needed and, having flown its last Spitfire V sorties on 4 July, the squadron carried out its first Mk.IX sorties on the 6th. By that time, 350 was still under ADGB authority and had moved to Westhampnett. In July convoy patrols made up the majority of operational sorties, but some Ramrods were carried out over Normandy. More than 300 sorties were flown in July, all being uneventful. Despite this, 350 was not spared drama. This second association with the Mk.IX was marred by the death of a British pilot as early as the 8th. Five Spitfires had taken off for formation practice that day when white smoke, coming from the right side of the cowling of the Spitfire flown by Sgt J. Wooley, was seen by F/O R. Duchâteau just before a round object flew off the left side followed by an explosion. Before disintegrating, the Spitfire became a mass of fire from the nose to tail. Wooley had no time to bale out. An engine failure was the cause

Spitfire ML137/MN-Z was the regular mount of F/L G. de Patoul who was at the end of his tour in July 1944; he was serving 350 since September 1942. He would return to 350 in April 1945 and shot down soon after on the 24th to spend the last days of the war as a PoW. The aircraft had the standard markings of the time although the spinner had the Belgian roundel painted on it. *(André Bar)*

of the loss of another Spitfire five days later, once more during a practice flight. Unable to re-start his engine, F/O P. Delorme crashed the aircraft on the edge of the aerodrome. While levelling out, he struck an anti-glider obstruction and overturned. The Spitfire was only good for scrap, but the pilot escaped with slight injuries. In August, news was received that 350 Squadron would participate in the anti-diver campaign and would re-equip with the Griffon-engine Spitfire XIV. The squadron continued to fly ops in the first week of August, close to 150 sorties being flown that week. On the evening of the 8th, the unit moved back to Hawkinge where it flew its last Spitfire IX ops the next day, an escort of Bostons to the Rouen area. Then, 350 opened a new chapter with its new Spitfire XIVs.

It was a remarkably quick process with the first operational patrols carried out on the afternoon of the 10th. At that time, the Spitfire XIVs allocated to 350 were: NH661/R, NH692, NH695, NH696/J, NH711, NH718, RM655/X, RM675/W, RM693/S, RM696, RM700/B, RM701/O, RM732, RM740, RM741/F, RM748/Z, RM750/P, RM753/N, RM754/G, RM756/Y, and RM760/E, but others were taken on charge in the days that followed. The first success against V-1s was recorded on 15 August when F/O R. Vanderveken and Sgt H.A. Boels shared in the destruction of a V-1 in the Ashford area early that morning. The next day, two more V-1s were shot down, one in the morning and the second late in the evening (the latter being shared between two Belgian pilots). On 19 August, 350 was sent on a Ranger over occupied Belgium in the Brussels/Saint-Trond/Chievre area. The take off was set early in the morning. Reaching Etterbeck, on the outskirts of Brussels, at zero feet, F/L A. Plisnier sighted a Ju88 (reported as a Ju188) about one mile away at 11 o'clock. He turned toward the Junkers and fired a short burst at about 60° and 600 yards. The Ju88 sighted him and a good dogfight started. Plisnier understood that, owing to his speed (about 300 mph), he could not turn inside the Junkers so he climbed to 3000 feet, made a long 15° astern attack, and fired a number of successive bursts, all from less than 150 yards and closing sometimes to 75 yards. He saw strikes on the inner wings and two yellow flashes behind the cockpit. Plisnier encountered rather accurate flak, but the dogfight continued at zero feet, sometimes between trees and chimneys. Finally he broke away thinking he had run out of ammunition. He then saw the enemy aircraft put its flaps down and enter a right hand turn. Plisnier came alongside, waggled his wings twice and peeled off. The Ju88 was trying to land in a small field, but, when flying over a hedge, the right wing dropped and the aircraft crashed. The day was a very successful one as, late in the day, while the squadron continued its anti-Diver patrols, one V-1 in the morning, and another in the afternoon, were added to the scoreboard. These were followed by a claim by F/Sgt P. Leva who tipped the V-1 with his right wing, causing it to crash and explode. The Spitfire returned safely to base albeit with a bent wingtip. This was the last V-1 claimed by 350 before it switched to escort duties from the 25th. That day, the Belgians flew two Ramrods, No. 1227 in the morning and No. 1230 in the afternoon, both having Amiens as the target. The operations were uneventful as were the next ones flown, a fighter sweep, a Ranger, but a mass Rhubarb saw two locos and eight lorries destroyed The next day Spitfire RM751 was destroyed when it caught fire during start up, but the pilot, F/Sgt J. Laloux, managed to evacuate his aircraft safely. The Spitfire was eventually struck off charge on 30 September after an investigation. The rest of August was quiet, but since the conversion 350 had flown close to 500 sorties on its new aircraft.

RM693/MN-S, one of the first Spitfire XIVs issued to 350 Sqn, was flown by various pilots, including S/L Donnet. This aircraft participated in the first sorties carried out. It later served with Nos. 130 and 41 Squadrons during the war. *(André Bar)*

Pilots of 350 Sqn gathered around their new mount in August 1944:
Left to right: Flying Officers J. Brosteaux, J. Wustefeld, P. Pacco, R. Vanderveken, and J. Vanderperren (†25.12.44), F/Sgt R. Méhuys, Sgt L. Lambrechts, S/L M. Donnet (CO), F/Sgt J. Laloux, F/L J. Lavigne (B Flight CO), Flying Officers A. Van Wersch and R. Duchâteau, P/O R. Bladt and F/O P. Delorme.
On the wing: Sergeants G. Gigot and M. Doncq. On the engine: Sgt R. Huens (†23.01.45), F/Sgt M. Morel (†11.11.44), F/O R. Muls and Sgt H. Boels. On the right wing: Sgt A. Kicq, F/O P. Siroux, F/L H. Smets (supernumerary), F/L R. Hoornaert (supernumerary) and F/O A. Claesen, the latter was visiting his former unit (he was instructing at 53 OTU at the time). Some pilots, like the A Flight CO, F/L A. Plisnier, were not present that day.
(André Bar)

September started intensively with 24 sorties flown on the 1st. An escort of Lancasters to the south of Lille became a mass Rhubarb during which a car and two locos were destroyed. In the afternoon another mass Rhubarb was carried with similar success: a staff car, two lorries, two flamers and two eight-wheel trucks were destroyed. At base, a V-1 hit by flak fell outside a dispersal bay and damaged three aircraft. One, RM695, was never repaired and struck off charge. Ops continued over the few next days without major incident. On the 5th, the squadron flew over the Belgian capital. The CO dropped a Belgian flag signed by all the pilots of 350. Between 7 and 9 September the weather was so bad that no flying was performed. Operations resumed on the 10th with an anti-Big Ben (the codename for hunting V-2 launch sites) op around Rotterdam. The rest of the month was spent on bomber escorts, armed recces or further Big Ben sorties. In all the squadron flew about 300 sorties in September, the last days being flown from Lympne where 130 and 350 Squadron exchanged their Spitfire XIVs, 130 joining 2 TAF on the Continent. The trade was a bad one for the Belgians as 130 Squadron's aircraft were found to be less well maintained. Operations from Lympne started on 2 October with a Ramrod escorting Mitchells to Arnhem, but over the next two days the weather deteriorated and prevented operational flying. On the 5th, the pilots were notified (the unit had been rife with rumours beforehand) that 350 was assigned to 2 TAF on the Continent. In the meantime operations from Lympne continued with Ramrods on the 6th, 7th, 14th and 25th (the days between being hampered by bad weather and a change of command on the 23rd with F/L L. Collignon taking over). All ops were completed without major incident except the last one as five Spitfires were posted missing on return. For various reasons the five missing Spitfires landed on the Continent, Flight Lieutenant A. Plisnier and P/O P. Paco made a safe landing at Brussels, F/Sgt E. Pauwels at Grimbergen (B.60), and F/Sgt M. Morel at Anvers-Durne (B.70) while F/Sgt L. Lambrechts had to belly land in a field short of petrol, wrecking his Spitfire in the process. All were back with the squadron before the month was done. Morel, being the last to re-join on the 31st, was therefore unable to participate in the last ops of the month. These were two bomber escorts on the 28th and another on the 30th. Owing to bad weather, which prevailed for most of October, 350 did not achieve a good operational record, with only about ninety sorties flown, but November was worse with 75 sorties flown across the eight days when the weather eased. In November, the squadron recorded two operational losses, the first on the 4th when, during an escort for Lancasters, the new CO was unable to switch to his main tank (from his belly tank). That obliged him to make a forced landing in an open field in Belgium. He was safe, but the aircraft was only good for scrap. He was back at the squadron the next day. The second loss occurred on the 14th. Flying Officer F. Verpoorten and F/Sgt L. Lambrechts took off that day, for an escort to Juvincourt, and landed at Amiens (B.48). Verpoorten missed his landing and collided with barracks at the end of the runway. This was the last flight of RM671, but Verpoorten was safe. To these

A line-up of 350 Squadron's Spitfire XIVs at dispersal at Hawkinge with RM748/MN-Z clearly visible. *(André Bar)*

Flying Officer J. Wustefeld standing on the wing of a Spitfire XIV. Wustefeld fled Belgium in June 1940 and was initially incorporated into the Belgian Army in England before being transferred to the RAF in September 1941. He survived the war and returned to civilian life after the war. Behind is a line-up of the unit's Spitfire XIVs with RB169/MN-F in the foreground. *(André Bar)*

two losses must be added the death of F/Sgt M. Morel on the 11th during a training flight. November was a black month for the Belgians with few operations flown to compensate. Only one op was carried from Lympne, a Ramrod to Bonheim on the 3rd, but the squadron was obliged to land at Evere (B.56) on the return journey because of the bad weather. While not ideal, this proved fortuitous as the squadron was planning to move there within days. Therefore, from that date, 350 operated from Evere. The squadron was placed under 127 Wing's authority and led by W/C 'Johnnie' Johnson. No operation was flown before the 8th because of the weather, but 350 flew various patrols, the last taking off at 15.00. No one returned from this patrol. Flight Lieutenant G. Seydel and F/O R. Duchâteau landed at B.67 (Ursel), while P/O M. Doncq and F/Sgt R. Jaminé crashed, short of petrol, in an open field near Maldegem. Jamine's aircraft was so badly damaged that no repairs were undertaken. Over the following days, 350 flew patrols and some fighter sweeps during which the Belgians were introduced to American anti-aircraft batteries which fired at the Belgians during a fighter patrol near Aachen. Two aircraft were damaged, but they and their pilots (F/Os R. Muls and A. Van Eeckhoudt) were able to return to base without further problems. Later in the day, F/L R. Hoornaert experienced an engine failure obliging him to make a forced landing just on the Allied side of the front. He was rescued by the Americans and was back at the squadron before the end of the day. Less than a week later, the CO, while on patrol over the Houffalize-Malmedy area, was hit by flak after making a pass at a flak position. He managed to return over Allied-held territory before he baled out at low altitude, breaking his leg badly. He would be evacuated to a Hospital in England on 25 December 1944 and saw no further operational actions during the War. Two other Spitfires were also damaged that day, but less seriously. The next day an armed recce was flown over the Malmedy-St-Vith area. A column of lorries was strafed, but unfortunately the aircraft flown by F/O J. Vanderperren was hit by debris from an exploding lorry (probably full of ammunition) and was seen to crash in flames. During the attack the Belgians claimed seven lorries destroyed. On 31 December 350 made another move, this time to Y.32 (Ash-Ophoven).

The new base was among the Operation Bodenplatte targets on 1 January 1945 when the Luftwaffe sent fighters to attack Allied bases to try to regain an advantage. One of the squadron's Spitfires was destroyed and another damaged on the ground. This attack did not disrupt the Allies that much and they were able to continue to carry out operations from that day even though many aircraft were temporarily unserviceable (350 Squadron was not totally operational). The weather actually had more of an effect on operations. On 4 January a new CO, S/L T. Spencer, arrived to assume command. He was formerly a flight commander with 41 Squadron. Meanwhile, as the number of aircraft to be repaired was so high within 2 TAF, a clever solution to make up losses was to send pilots to the UK to collect replacements. Eleven were sent to Tangmere, but they had to wait for the weather to improve to return to the Continent. There was no let up until the 12th. Little in the way of operational activity was carried out by the remaining pilots, but

Terry Spencer initially served with the British Army before being transferred to the RAF in the autumn of 1941. Once his training was completed, he served as an army co-operation pilot flying Mustangs with No. 26 Squadron. It was not until February 1944 that he began work as a fighter pilot when he was posted to No. 165 Squadron as a flight commander. He then moved to No. 41 Squadron where he converted to the Spitfire Mk.XII, the first operational Griffon-powered Spitfire, and participated in the V-1 campaign during the summer of 1944, claiming eight 'buzz bombs' destroyed. On 3 September 1944, he destroyed an Fw190, his only claim over a manned aircraft. In December 1944, Spencer was given command of No. 350 (Belgian) Squadron until 26 February 1945 when he was shot down and became a PoW. However, he managed to escape and was back at the squadron a couple of weeks later, resuming command in mid-April, but was shot down the following week to become a PoW once again. He was liberated about a fortnight later and left the RAF in December 1945, having been awarded a DFC in June.

Supermarine Spitfire Mk.XIV NH689
No. 350 (Belgian) Squadron
Squadron Leader T. Spencer
Y.32/Ophoven (Belgium), January 1945

it must be said the weather did not help. On 14 January S/L Spencer led the Belgians for the first time, participating in a fighter sweep around St-Vith where a large concentration of vehicles was shot up. The squadron claimed the highest score of the Wing. Twoe next days later an armed reconnaissance was led by the wing leader, the Canadian W/C G.C. Keefer. This operation was not as successful as the previous one as the squadron flew into walls of flak and F/L H. Smets' Spitfire hit badly enough to force him to bale out into captivity. No operations were flown until the 22nd because the runway was flooded. On the 22nd, the squadron provided two patrols of two aircraft each for the entire day over Bese Weert and Nygemen Volkel . That day each pilot flew twice, some of them three times. The following day, armed recces were carried out all day long and while various targets of opportunity were strafed, flak was again accurate, shooting down and killing F/Sgt R. Huens. Flying low, he didn't have time to evacuate his aircraft. Armed recces continued until the end of the month, increasing the scoreboard with lorries, locos and other ground targets destroyed, without any loss to record. The squadron moved to B.78/Eindhoven on 27 January, its new home for the next two months. In February, the number of sorties more than doubled, 290 performed in all. The main task remained armed recces or patrols, as far as weather permitted, and the Belgians found many opportunities to strafe targets on the ground, but flak took its toll when F/Sgt J. Laloux was shot down around Osnabrück on the 11th and was captured. On 21 February, the Belgians escorted bombers targeting Weese. That was followed by an uneventful fighter sweep over the Rhine. That was not the case for the next one late in the afternoon. The squadron met a formation of twenty enemy fighters. The Belgians had just reformed above cloud after several pilots had chased some Me262s without result. At around 17.30, the squadron was close to Rheine aerodrome when P/O L. Lambrechts saw a Bf109 at about 600-700 feet. There was a dogfight going on and, as he went after the Bf109, the German pilot pulled up and went above the cloud, which was between 7-8/10ths at 5000 feet with clear patches. Lambrecht went after him and closed in to about 75-100 yards. He was dead astern when he opened fire with all guns. He saw strikes all over the cockpit and fuselage and the Bf109 rolled on its back and, smoking badly, dived vertically out of control. Soon after, Lambrecht saw two more Bf109s at 3000 feet. One of them was chasing F/Sgt C. Brahy. Quickly, he managed to get behind this Bf109 and opened fire from about 500 yards dead astern, closing until the enemy aircraft broke away. He saw strikes on the left wing. He could not go further because he had no ammunition left and also because another Bf109 was attacking him. He pulled up and left the area. Lambrechts claimed one Bf109 destroyed and another damaged on return, but his first was later adjusted to probably destroyed. He was not the only one to score in this engagement. Flight Lieutenant J. Lavigne did too, with one Bf109 destroyed, as did F/O A. Van Wersch, while Brahy claimed one damaged. The squadron returned to its armed recce work over the following days with an escort, that ended as a fighter sweep, thrown in for good measure. On 26 February 350 carried out Rhubarbs all day over the Rheine area, but their British CO was hit by flak and had to abandon his aircraft. He was a PoW for a short time as, five weeks later in March, he managed to escape and evade. The two ops on 1 March were uneventful. The next day, W/C G.C. Keefer and 350 participated in a fighter sweep over Rheine as the first operation of the day. German aircraft were reported by control, when the Wing was near Eschede, so the Spitfires turned towards Rheine. Wing Commander Keefer, who was flying with 130 Squadron, led them down while 350 remained as top cover. Keefer's formation was soon involved in a dogfight and the section led by F/L R. Hoornaert came to the rescue (Hoornaert was leading P/O L. Lambrechts, and Flight Sergeants J. Groensteen and F/Sgt E. Pauwels). Pauwels claimed a Bf109 as damaged while the other three put in claims for one destroyed each. The next day S/L Spencer's successor, S/L F.G. Woolley, arrived and was

Spitfire NH689/MN-B at a snowy Y32/Ophoven in January 1945. It was S/L Spencer's mount at the time. The fuselage band has been overpainted to obey to the new 2 TAF regulation of 3 January 1945 but the underwing roundel has yet to be modified. *(André Bar)*

Harold Edward WALMSLEY

'Harry' Walmsley joined the RAF in December 1940. However, he had to wait some months to commence flying training, being one of the first pupils to be sent to Rhodesia. He returned to the UK in June 1942 where he attended 61 OTU. In September, he was posted to No. 611 (County of Lincolnshire) Squadron as a NCO. He made his first claim, a probable Fw190, on 9 January 1943, receiving his commission the same month. His score continued to increase and in August 1943 he was posted to No. 132 (City of Bombay) Squadron as a flight commander. With 132 he added further claims before seeing his tour come to an end in April 1944 and earning a DFC in the process.

He returned to operations in October 1944 with No. 130 (Punjab) Squadron, now flying the Griffon-powered Spitfire Mk.XIV. He in-creased his tally significantly during the winter. In April 1945, he was given command of No. 350 (Belgian) Squadron, still flying Spitfire XIVs, a unit with which he made his final claims. The very last one, a Fw190 shared destroyed on 26 April, brought his score to eleven confirmed victories (one shared), one probable and four damaged. In July 1945, he added a Bar to his DFC. He continued to serve in the RAF until 1971 when he retired as a Group Captain.

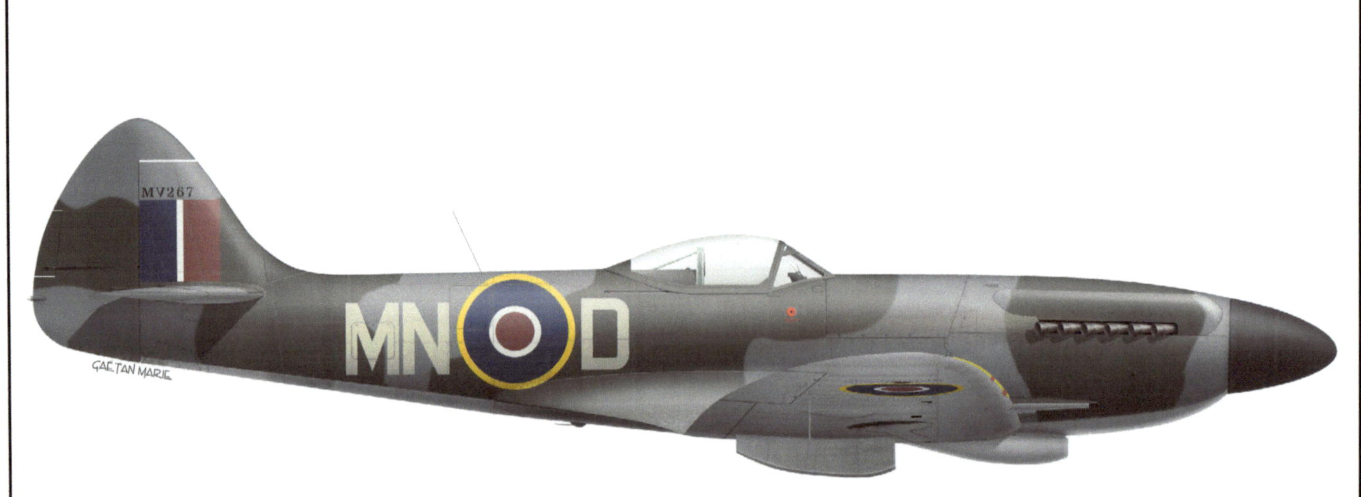

Supermarine Spitfire Mk.XIV MV267
No. 350 (Belgian) Squadron
B.172/Husum (Germany), June-July 1945

immediately on the job leading 350 in operations during the day and the busy few days that followed. On 13 March, he was leading an escort for Marauders when he saw a group of about twenty aircraft flying in the opposite direction. He went after them with his section and it took about two minutes at full throttle to catch up while still not being certain of their identity. He attempted to pull up alongside the outside aircraft on the right side. That aircraft turned into him and Woolley recognised it as a Fw190. Woolley got on to its tail and the Fw190 climbed up into a layer of thin cloud. He opened fire from dead astern at 100 yards, seeing many strikes on the wing roots and fuselage. The aircraft then burst into flames from the left wing root and base of the cockpit. Woolley had to break sharply away to avoid flying through debris. A few days later, 350 packed their things to return to England, to Warmwell, for an Air Firing course. They remained at Warmwell until 1 April, when released from the course, and were back at Eindhoven the next day. Their return coincided with S/L T. Spencer's homecoming after five weeks of captivity and an outstanding escape. On the 3rd, 350 took off twice for armed recces, but could not get through because of bad weather. The following day was most successful with an armed recce to Linden and Quakenbruck in the morning, during which a few lorries and horse carts were destroyed or damaged, and an armed recce mounted in the afternoon. Unfortunately, the flak was accurate and hit the Spitfire flown by F/L R. Hoornaert. He was obliged to make a forced landing near Meppen and spent what was left of the war as a PoW. The next day, the squadron returned to the same area. Flying Officer R. Muls, after having shot up a horse cart, was attacked by a Fw190 with a long nose. He avoided the initial attacked and got in position to fire at the Fw190D, seeing strikes on the fuselage. The Fw190 rolled on its back. Muls followed him, still firing, and was forced to break up to avoid a collision. He then received some backup from his wingman, F/Sgt S. Neulinger, who finished off the enemy aircraft, the German pilot eventually jumping out of his aircraft. The claim was shared by the two pilots. The Belgians returned with one of their own missing, however, as P/O A. Creswell-Turner had been shot down earlier, probably by the same Fw190D. The British pilot survived as a PoW. Two days later, 350 moved to Germany, B.106/Twente, from where operations began at once with patrols and armed recces. Flak remained the main danger and, in the Wihelmshaven-Emden area, F/Sgt G. Gigot was hit by flak. His wing exploded and his Glycol system began to leak, but, by some kind of miracle, he succeeded in returning close to base where the engine cut out and he landed a few hundred yards off the runway. Despite considerable damage, the Spitfire was repaired. Two days later it was the turn of P/O R. François to be hit by flak, receiving a 40mm shell in the fuselage. Like Gigot, he managed to reach base. On the 15th F/Sgt J. Van Liefland had to land at B.110, after his aircraft was hit by flak, but collided with an Auster. The aircraft was only good for scrap, but Van Leifland returned to the squadron. Previously, on 12 April, S/L Woolley had left to take command of 130 Squadron, allowing S/L Spencer to regain the position he had vacated in February when he was shot down. On 17 April, 350 made another move forward to B.118/Celle. This new base brought some luck for the Belgians when, after having seen one of their own lost in the morning (F/O M. Doncq was hit by flak, damaging an aileron, but he returned to base), F/Sgt A. Kicq shot down a Fw190D shortly after he bombed a tug southeast of Hamburg that afternoon. In the evening, the squadron performed a sweep over Berlin, but found little of interest if we ignore the symbolic side of the flight. Armed recces continued, mainly in the Lubeck-Hambourg area, and targets of opportunity were attacked when found. On 19 April, in the evening, 350 carried out a sweep over Parchim- Güstrow-Wismar. The CO was shot down while attacking a small ship in the bay off Wismar. His aircraft was seen to explode, but, miraculously, he was ejected by the explosion and a chute was seen to open (setting a record for surviving the lowest bale out on record – 30 feet). He landed in the water where he was rescued by German sailors and transported to a hospital where he spent the rest of the war.

The squadron had its revenge the following day. It started badly for 350 as, during an armed recce over the Lubeck-Hamburg area in the late morning, F/L K. Smith (British) was shot down after flying into a flak trap. He was hit in the coolant system and made a forced landing near Schwerin. He was seen by his wingman, F/Sgt C. Orban de Xivry, getting out of the cockpit and walking towards the nearby woods. He evaded and returned to the squadron soon after on 4 May in a German staffcar. The blow was severe as in two days 350 had lost its CO and a Flight CO. The day was not over yet. Late in the evening, a sweep was flown in the Berlin area. In the Nauen area the formation encountered about twenty Fw190s flying in the opposite direction at a lower altitude. Combat was inevitable and the leader decided to attack with 350 immediately gaining the advantage over the Fw190s who lost five of their own to F/L D.R. Howorth, F/Sgt A. Kicq (and another probably destroyed), P/O R. Muls, F/O M. Doncq and P/O D.J. Watkins (British). However, two of the claims (Kicq's probably destroyed and Muls' victory) were later downgraded to damaged. The day ended much better than it started even if F/Sgt J. Groensteen was posted missing. The squadron's area of operations was restricted as the Soviets were entering Berlin for the final battle. All pilots received a special document, written in both English and Cyrillic, in case they had to make a forced landing in the Soviet lines. The next day, during a Wing sweep, led by G/C 'Johnnie' Johnson, 350 met Soviet aircraft for the first time (Yaks escorting the famous Shturmoviks). The squadron was led by the new CO, S/L H. Walmsley, who had just arrived from 130 Squadron. In the afternoon, while flying an armed recce in the Pritzwalk and Rostock area, F/O A. Van Eeckhoudt and P/O D.J. Watkins surprised a He111 heading north and following a road at ground level. Watkins was the first to attack, closing in and firing a quick burst at its left engine, which was hit. He had to break left to avoid debris. Albert Van Eeckhout followed and fired a long burst. The He111 then crash landed in a nearby field. The claim was shared. Later in the evening, the new CO was leading six aircraft on a fighter sweep over the Wismar-Parchim area when, approaching Wismar at 6000 feet, enemy aircraft were reported on the reciprocal heading at 7000 feet. They managed to get around behind the formation and started the chase. The enemy aircraft climbed into cloud and Walmsley ordered one of his sections to go above the cloud while he led his section into cloud. Walmsley found one Fw190 ahead of him. When the German realised he was being chased he dived through cloud to about 3500 feet. Walmsley followed it and fired two long-range bursts, but did not notice any results. At 2000 feet the Fw190 levelled out, slowed down and lowered its undercarriage as it approached Kleinen airfield. Walmsley got on its tail and fired a two second burst from directly astern. The Fw190 blew up and crashed in flames. Flight Lieutenant G. de Patoul claimed another Fw190 probably destroyed, but fell victim to an engine failure and had to abandon his aircraft. Captured, he was the last of the squadron's wartime losses. During the last days of April 1945, pressure was increased and as many armed recces as possible were flown as Nazi Germany collapsed. As each hour passed, however, the area to attack became more and more restricted as the Soviets advanced towards the west and the Allied lines. Despite this the Luftwaffe was continuing to fight and encounters became more frequent as German airspace shrunk. Around midday, during an armed recce, about twenty Fw190s were encountered around the airfield of Rechlin and, without difficulty, 350 claimed three destroyed, including two by P/O E. Pauwels, while F/O P. Delorme claimed another damaged, the third Fw190 destroyed being credited to the CO. The next day, the squadron scored again against

A line-up of 350 Squadron's Spitfire XIVs at Fassberg on 5 May 1945. In the forefront NH654/MN-X and behind RM869/MN-V and RN198/MN-T
(André Bar)

Fw190s. Flight Sergeant G. Gigot sealed the fate of one while a second was shared by a group of four pilots that included the CO. This Fw190 was credited without the four pilots having to fire a single shot as it stalled as it tried to escape, the German pilot jumping out while his aircraft spun and crashed into the ground. Patrols and armed recces continued over the following days and were uneventful until the last day of the month. That day the squadron patrolled in the Wittenburg-Haguenau-Ludwiglust area. Around 10.45, the patrol – consisting of F/L P. Bangerter (British), P/O D.J. Watkins and F/Sgt G. Gigot – caught roughly twenty Fw190s about to land in an airstrip. Carnage followed as the German fighters were caught low and slow. Bangerter claimed two, as did Watkins, while F/Sgt Gigot destroyed one and a sixth was shared between the three pilots. That's how April, with the squadron flying 550 sorties for the month, ended.

By May, it was clear the war in Europe was in its last days, but encounters with the Luftwaffe continued. On 1 May, 28 patrols were flown and in the evening, near Schwerin Lake, about twenty enemy aircraft were sighted flying at zero feet. Not identified at first, the Belgians, led by F/L R. Muls, came down from 10,000 feet to confirm a formation of Fw190s flying in sections of three. Flying Officer P. Leva selected the leading section and lined up the aircraft flying on the left side. He overshot owing to his diving speed, however, but, after climbing slightly to lose speed, he came in again behind the same Fw190. When within 300 yards, he fired a half second burst from 10° deflection without noticing any strikes. At the same time he observed he was closer to the middle aircraft of the section, so he got in behind it and fired a three second burst from 150 yards dead astern. He saw two explosions, one on each side of the fuselage. The Fw190 started to climb steeply to the right and Leva followed it and saw the German pilot jettison his hood, roll the aircraft on its back, and bale out at 1000 feet. Leva was the first to make a claim, but he was soon followed by F/Sgt H. Boels, who made two, and F/L R. Muls (one). The next day, an Arado 234 jet bomber was caught by surprise, as it was landing at Hohn aerodrome, and was shot down. Its destruction was shared by the four pilots of the section. This was the squadron's final aerial victory. Later in the evening, F/O P. Leva came close to being the unit's last casualty when he was hit by flak and the Spitfire caught fire. Miraculously, the fire went out and Leva was able to make it back to base safely. Patrols and armed recces continued over the next three days. The last were completed in the early hours of the 5th with no further ops necessary as the German forces in the north had capitulated on the 4th (effective from the 5th at 08.00). The squadron moved to B.152/Fassberg the next day. It stayed in Germany to become part of the occupying forces, moving to B.72/Husum on 21 June, B.116/Wunstorf on 13 July, and returning to B.152 Fassberg on 29 November. During that period of time, air activity was reduced, but two Spitfires were wrecked, the first on 9 June 1945 when the engine caught fire on start up, and the second on 17 December when it swung on take off onto soft ground and tipped over. The aircraft was not repaired as the RAF had too many Spitfires with the MUs. The Belgians swapped their Mk.XIVs for XVIs in August 1946, 350 having seen a new CO posted in in the meantime, S/L R. Van Lierde. The squadron was eventually transferred to the control of the Belgian Air Force on 15 October 1946. Just before the transfer, 350 experienced its last lost as an RAF unit when a Spitfire XVI made a forced-landing at Darup 15 miles west of Münster following an engine failure during a communication flight. The pilot, Wing Commander L. Prévot being slightly injured in the process.

Date	Pilot	SN	Origin	Type	Serial	Code	Nb	Cat.
				SPITFIRE Mk V				
19.05.42	Sgt Jean ESTER	RAF No. 1299910	(BEL)/RAF	Bf109	**BL622**	MN-A	1.0	P
23.05.42	P/O André PLISNIER	RAF No. 100654	(BEL)/RAF	Fw190	**AD573**	MN-C	1.0	C
01.06.42	F/L Yvan DU MONCEAU DE B.	RAF No. 87700	(BEL)/RAF	Fw190	**BL540**	MN-Y	1.0	C
29.06.42	P/O Henri PICARD	RAF No.87693	(BEL)/RAF	Fw190	**EN796**	MN-D	2.0	C
30.07.42	F/L Yvan DU MONCEAU DE B.	RAF No. 87700	(BEL)/RAF	Bf109	**EN794**	MN-X	1.0	P
	P/O Henri MARCHAL	RAF No. 87678	(BEL)/RAF	Bf109	**BM176**	MN-M	0.5	C
	Sgt Jean ESTER	RAF No. 1299910	(BEL)/RAF		**EN796**	MN-D	0.5	C
19.08.42	F/L Yvan DU MONCEAU DE B.	RAF No. 87700	(BEL)/RAF	Fw190	**EN794**	MN-X	1.0	C
	P/O Henri PICARD	RAF No. 87693	(BEL)/RAF	Fw190	**BM297**		0.5	C
	P/O Emile PLAS	RAF No. 87697	(BEL)/RAF		**AB912**		0.5	C
	Sgt Robert ALEXANDRE	RAF No. 1299925	(BEL)/RAF	Fw190	**W3646**	MN-V	1.0	P
	F/L Adolphe BOUSSA	RAF No. 101465	(BEL)/RAF	Fw190	**EN769**	MN-G	1.0	C
	P/O François VENESOEN	RAF No. 107235	(BEL)/RAF	Fw190	**AD475**	MN-S	1.0	C
	P/O Herman SMETS	RAF No. 87694	(BEL)/RAF	Ju88	**BM240**	MN-B	0.25	C
	Sgt Frédéric BOUTE	RAF No. 1395131	(BEL)/RAF		**BM230**	MN-F	0.25	C
	P/O André PLISNIER	RAF No. 100654	(BEL)/RAF	Fw190	**BM564**	MN-J	0.25	C
	Sgt Jean VANLERBERGHE	RAF No. 1299891	(BEL)/RAF	Fw190	**AD475**	MN-S	0.25	C
	P/O André PLISNIER	RAF No. 100654	(BEL)/RAF	Fw190	**BM564**	MN-J	1.0	C
	P/O François VENESOEN	RAF No. 107235	(BEL)/RAF	Fw190	**AD475**	MN-S	1.0	C
27.08.42	F/L Yvan DU MONCEAU DE B.	RAF No. 87700	(BEL)/RAF	Fw190	**EN794**	MN-Y	1.0	C
	P/O Emile PLAS	RAF No. 87697	(BEL)/RAF	Fw190	**BM240**	MN-B	1.0	P
16.11.42	P/O André PLISNIER	RAF No. 100654	(BEL)/RAF	Ju52	**BM564**	MN-J	0.50	C
	P/O François VENESOEN	RAF No. 107235	(BEL)/RAF		**AD231**	MN-A	0.50	C
19.11.42	P/O André PLISNIER	RAF No. 100654	(BEL)/RAF	Bf110	**BM564**	MN-J	0.50	C
	Sgt Léon HARMEL	RAF No. 1299917	(BEL)/RAF		**P8549**	MN-L	0.50	C
22.01.43	P/O Robert ALEXANDRE	RAF No. 134055	(BEL)/RAF	Fw190	**EE745**	MN-N	1.0	C
	P/O André PLISNIER	RAF No. 100654	(BEL)/RAF	Fw190	**EE753**	MN-X	1.0	P
06.04.43	F/L Adolphe BOUSSA	RAF No. 101465	(BEL)/RAF	Do217	**BM428**	MN-H	1.0	C
21.12.43	F/O Albert HERREMAN	RAF No. 146066	(BEL)/RAF	Fw190	**EN854**	MN-A	1.0	C
28.12.43	F/O Paul SIROUX	RAF No. 127853	(BEL)/RAF	Fw190	**AB875**		1.0	C
				SPITFIRE Mk XIV				
15.08.44	Sgt Hendrik BOELS	RAF No. 1424945	(BEL)/RAF	V-1	**RM748**	MN-Z	0.5	C
	F/O Robert VANDERVEKEN	RAF No. 147775	(BEL)/RAF		**RM655**	MN-X	0.5	C
16.08.44	F/Sgt Louis VERBEECK	RAF No. 1299865	(BEL)/RAF	V-1	**RM655**	MN-X	1.0	C
	P/O Jean LAVIGNE	RAF No. 156374	(BEL)/RAF	V-1	**RM701**	MN-O	0.5	C
	Sgt Paul LEVA	RAF No. 1299863	(BEL)/RAF		**RM693**	MN-S	0.5	C
19.08.44	F/L André PLISNIER	RAF No. 100654	(BEL)/RAF	Ju188	**RM754**	MN-G	1.0	C
	F/O Jacques WUSTEFELD	RAF No. 169984	(BEL)/RAF	V-1	**RM760**	MN-E	1.0	C
	F/Sgt Louis VERBEECK	RAF No. 1299865	(BEL)/RAF	V-1	**RM760**	MN-E	1.0	C
20.08.44	Sgt Paul LEVA	RAF No. 1299863	(BEL)/RAF	V-1	**RM701**	MN-O	1.0	C
21.02.45	P/O Ludovic LAMBRECHTS	RAF No. 186091	(BEL)/RAF	Bf109	**RM618**	MN-P	1.0	P

André Plisnier
RAF No. 100654

'Plis' Plisnier enlisted in the Belgian Army in August 1939. In March 1940, he volunteered for pilot training, which he had not completed when Belgium was invaded in May. He followed his flying school to France, then to French Morocco, eventually making his way to the UK in August. Here he enlisted in the RAF and completed his training. In April 1941, he attended 58 OTU, being posted to No. 131 (County of Kent) Squadron, in which a Belgian flight had been formed, in July. Naturally, when this flight was raised as No. 350 (Belgian) Squadron in November, he became one of its founding members. 'Plis' opened his score the following 23 May when he claimed an Fw190 destroyed over the Saint-Omer–Calais area. More claims followed until he was posted out for a rest in February 1943. He received the DFC in September. In April 1944, he re-joined 350 for another tour and, on 19 August 1944, claimed a Ju88 destroyed, bringing his tally to six confirmed victories (three shared), one probable and three damaged. He was one of the few Belgian aces of WW2. From November 1944 to January 1945, 'Plis' was attached to the 336th Fighter Group, flying Mustangs with the Americans, again becoming a rarity among his countrymen by being one of the few Belgian pilots to have flown the Mustang operationally during the war. He survived the war and was discharged from the RAF in June 1946.

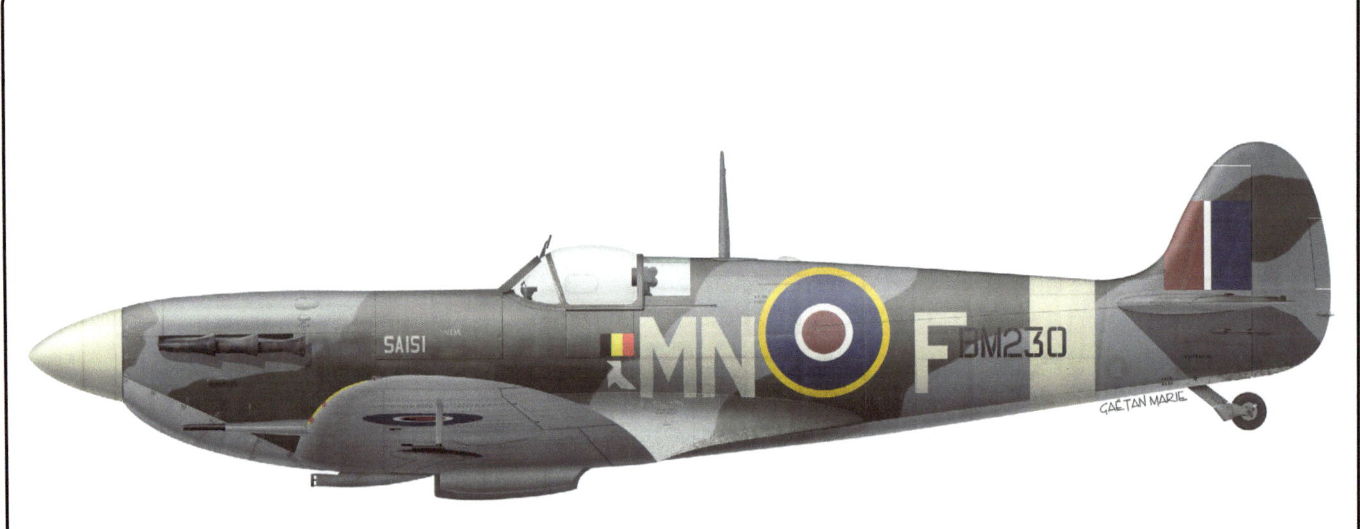

Supermarine Spitfire Mk.VB BM230
No. 350 (Belgian) Squadron
Redhill (UK), June 1942

François Venesoen
RAF No. 107235

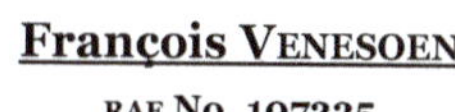

'Sus' Venesoen enlisted in the *Aéronautique Militaire* in March as a pilot but failed his initial training; he was then re-mustered as an air gunner in May. One year later, when the Germans invaded the country, he was an air gunner on Fairey Foxes, in which he participated in the initial skirmishes, before being evacuated to France and then sailing to the UK, arriving on 23 June. He enlisted in the RAF and, in August, was posted to No. 235 Squadron as an air gunner on Blenheim Mk.IVFs. In November, 'Sus' was posted to No. 272 Squadron, but his stay was brief as his application for pilot training had been accepted. At the end of 1941, training complete, he was posted to No. 350 (Belgian) Squadron. He made his first claims over Dieppe the following 19 August, claiming two Fw190s destroyed over the city. In March 1943, 350 moved north for a rest but Venesoen remained on the front line and was posted to No. 610 (County of Chester) Squadron. With this unit he made his last claim, a Bf110 shared destroyed, on 24 September to bring his scoreboard to five confirmed victories (two shared). A DFC followed in December as his tour came to an end. In May 1944, he re-joined 350 for another tour but on D-Day his Spitfire suffered an engine failure and he was obliged to bale out over the Channel. François Venesoen was never found.

Supermarine Spitfire Mk.VC EE766
No. 350 (Belgian) Squadron
Fairlop (UK), March 1943

Date	Pilot	Service No.	Nationality	Aircraft	Serial	Code	Score	Type
	F/L Jean **Lavigne**	RAF No. 156374	(BEL)/RAF	Bf109	**RM729**	MN-M	1.0	C
	P/O Albert **Van Wersch**	RAF No. 169983	(BEL)/RAF	Bf109	**RM648**	MN-R	1.0	C
02.03.45	P/O Ludovic **Lambrechts**	RAF No. 186091	(BEL)/RAF	Bf109	**RM618**	MN-P	1.0	C
	F/Sgt Jacques **Groensteen**	RAF No. 1299851	(BEL)/RAF	Bf109	**RM648**	MN-R	1.0	C
	F/L Roger **Hoornaert**	RAF No. 128392	(BEL)/RAF	Bf109	**RB183**	MN-Z	1.0	C
13.03.45	S/L Frank G. **Woolley**	RAF No. 105174	RAF	Fw190	**NH686**	MN-V	1.0	C
05.04.45	F/O Robert **Muls**	RAF No. 153066	(BEL)/RAF	Fw190	**RB189**	MN-G	0.50	C
	F/Sgt Sigmund**Neulinger**	RAF No. 1424916	(BEL)/RAF	Fw190	**RB181**	MN-H	0.50	C
17.04.45	F/Sgt André **Kicq**	RAF No. 1424884	(BEL)/RAF	Fw190	**RB155**	MN-C	1.0	C
20.04.45	F/L David M. **Howorth**	RAF No. 82678	RAF	Fw190	**RM618**	MN-P	1.0	C
	F/O Marcel **Doncq**	RAF No. 182304	(BEL)/RAF	Fw190	**NH693**	MN-J	1.0	C
	F/Sgt André **Kicq**	RAF No. 1424884	(BEL)/RAF	Fw190	**RB181**	MN-H	1.0	C
	P/O Desmond J. **Watkins**	RAF No. 188502	RAF	Fw190	**RB155**	MN-C	1.0	C
24.04.45	F/O Albert **Van Eeckhoudt**	RAF No. 158777	(BEL)/RAF	He111	**NH697**	MN-K	0.50	C
	P/O Desmond J. **Watkins**	RAF No. 188502	RAF				0.50	C
	S/L Harold E. **Walmsley**	RAF No. 139425	RAF	Fw190	**SM825**	MN-M	1.0	C
	F/L Guy **de Patoul**	RAF No. 87684	(BEL)/RAF	Fw190	**RM618**	MN-P	1.0	P
25.04.45	S/L Harold E. **Walmsley**	RAF No. 139425	RAF	Fw190	**SM825**	MN-M	1.0	C
	P/O Émile **Pauwels**	RAF No. 195058	(BEL)/RAF	Fw190	**NH654**	MN-X	2.0	C
26.04.45	F/Sgt Guy **Gigot**	RAF No. 1424921	(BEL)/RAF	Fw190	**RB181**	MN-H	1.0	C
	S/L Harold E. **Walmsley**	RAF No. 139425	RAF	Fw190	**RN198**	MN-T	0.25	C
	F/Sgt Guy **Gigot**	RAF No. 1424921	(BEL)/RAF		**RB181**	MN-H	0.25	C
	P/O Paul **Leva**	RAF No. 186344	(BEL)/RAF				0.25	C
	F/O Marcel **Doncq**	RAF No. 182304	(BEL)/RAF	Fw190	**NH693**	MN-J	0.25	C
30.04.45	F/L Patrick M. **Bangerter**	RAF No. 124911	RAF	Fw190	**SM825**	MN-M	2.0	C
	P/O Desmond J. **Watkins**	RAF No. 188502	RAF	Fw190	**SM814**	MN-A	2.0	C
	F/Sgt Guy **Gigot**	RAF No. 1424921	(BEL)/RAF	Fw190	**NH689**	MN-B	1.0	C
	F/L Patrick M. **Bangerter**	RAF No. 124911	RAF	Fw190	**SM825**	MN-M	0.33	C
	P/O Desmond J. **Watkins**	RAF No. 188502	RAF	Fw190	**SM814**	MN-A	0.33	C
	F/Sgt Guy **Gigot**	RAF No. 1424921	(BEL)/RAF	Fw190	**NH689**	MN-B	0.33	C
01.05.45	P/O Paul **Leva**	RAF No. 186344	(BEL)/RAF	Fw190	**NH690**	MN-R	1.0	C
	F/Sgt Hendrik **Boels**	RAF No. 1424945	(BEL)/RAF	Fw190	**RM689**	MN-E	2.0	C
	F/L Robert **Muls**	RAF No. 153066	(BEL)/RAF	Fw190	**SM825**	MN-M	1.0	C
02.05.45	F/L Patrick M. **Bangerter**	RAF No. 124911	RAF	Ar234	**NH661**	MN-Y	0.25	C
	P/O Desmond J. **Watkins**	RAF No. 188502	RAF		**SM814**	MN-A	0.25	C
	F/O Albert **Van Eeckhoudt**	RAF No. 158777	(BEL)/RAF		**NH697**	MN-K	0.25	C
	F/Sgt André **Kicq**	RAF No. 1424884	(BEL)/RAF		**RB155**	MN-C	0.25	C

Total: 57.0 + 6.0 V-1

Some of the pilots of 350 Sqn who made claims during the final stages of the war. Above:

F/L D.M. Howorth, a British pilot, as was P/O D.J. Watkins. Both arrived at the squadron in March 1945 to reinforce the Belgians. Watkins had previously served with 132 Sqn. He was awarded the DFC in July 1945 for his service with 350.
Three Belgian pilots. Left, Pilot Officer E. Pauwels, who fled Belgium in March 1941, but was interned in Spain until March 1942 before making for the UK. He was posted to 350 Sqn in July 1944 as his first operational assignment. He survived the war. Flight Sergeant A. Kicq (below left) arrived at the squadron two weeks after Pauwels. He managed to escape Belgium in October 1941 and arrived in England in March 1942. Joining 350 Sqn in July 1944, he survived the war. Both flew for the Belgian airline SABENA after the war. Below right, Flight Sergeant 'Kéké' Gigot. He reached England in March 1942 after having been interned in Spain for six months. He would joined SABENA airlines as well after the war. *(André Bar)*

Date	Pilot	S/N	Origin	Serial	Code	Fate
		SPITFIRE Mk V				
30.04.42	P/O Georges **DELTOUR**	RAF No. 100651	(BEL)/RAF	**AA934**	MN-J	-
09.05.42	Sgt José **BLAIRON**	RAF No. 1299913	(BEL)/RAF	**AA857**	MN-K	†
19.05.42	Sgt Jean **ESTER**	RAF No. 1299910	(BEL)/RAF	**BL622**	MN-A	-
23.05.42	P/O Louis **PETEERS**	RAF No. 103566	(BEL)/RAF	**AR333**	MN-P	PoW
	P/O Etienne **WINTERBEEK**	RAF No. 87680	(BEL)/RAF	**BL476**	MN-E	†
01.06.42	W/C John G.A. **GORDON**	RAF No. 36075	(CAN)/RAF	**BL936**	MN-U	†
	P/O Robert **LAUMANS**	RAF No. 67088	(BEL)/RAF	**AB173**	MN-O	PoW
	F/Sgt Georges **LIVYNS**	RAF No. 1299900	(BEL)/RAF	**BL822**	MN-T	†
	Sgt José **HANSEZ**	RAF No. 1299901	(BEL)/RAF	**W3626**	MN-S	†
04.06.42	P/O Raymond **SCHROBILTGEN**	RAF No. 87696	(BEL)/RAF	**EN835**		†
13.06.42	Sgt Maurice **RAES**	RAF No. 1299915	(BEL)/RAF	**W3446**	MN-R	†
29.06.42	P/O Roger **DE WEVER**	RAF No. 87692	(BEL)/RAF	**AA835**	MN-E	PoW
05.08.42	P/O Gabriel **SEYDEL**	RAF No. 116541	(BEL)/RAF	**AD322**	MN-D	-
10.08.42	P/O Xavier **MENU**	RAF No. 87683	(BEL)/RAF	**W3214**	MN-F	†
13.08.42	P/O Raymond **DEHASSE**	RAF No. 117621	(BEL)/RAF	**EN769**	MN-G	-
16.08.42	Sgt Jean **ESTER**	RAF No. 1299910	(BEL)/RAF	**AB980**	MN-S	Eva.
19.08.42	P/O Henri **MARCHAL**	RAF No. 87678	(BEL)/RAF	**AR380**	MN-Z	-
27.08.42	P/O Henri **PICARD**	RAF No. 87693	(BEL)/RAF	**BM297**		PoW[1]
	P/O Martin **CHARLIER**	RAF No. 117620	(BEL)/RAF	**AB912**		†
21.09.42	P/O François **VENESOEN**	RAF No. 107235	(BEL)/RAF	**W3236**	MN-H	-
	Sgt Léopold **HEIMES**	RAF No. 1299983	(BEL)/RAF	**BM230**	MN-F	-
12.12.42	F/O Werner (Prince) **DE MÉRODE**	RAF No. 116473	(BEL)/RAF	**AD550**	MN-N	Eva.
22.01.43	Sgt Louis **FLOHIMONT**	RAF No. 1299902	(BEL)/RAF	**AR592**		†
13.11.43	F/Sgt Frédéric **BOUTE**	RAF No. 1395131	(BEL)/RAF	**EP240**	MN-C	†
	Sgt Michel **DE HEPCÉE**	RAF No. 1399178	(BEL)/RAF	**BM652**	MN-F	†
20.12.43	F/Sgt Léon **HARMEL**	RAF No. 1299917	(BEL)/RAF	**AD314**	MN-W	Eva.
28.12.43	F/Sgt Gaston **DANCOT**	RAF No. 1299847	(BEL)/RAF	**BM468**	MN-P	†
		SPITFIRE Mk IX				
30.01.44	P/O Georges **DUCHENE**	RAF No. 132975	(BEL)/RAF	**MH428**	MN-Z	†
	F/O Jean **GÉRARD**	RAF No. 132971	(BEL)/RAF	**MH476**	MN-F	†
		SPITFIRE Mk V				
30.04.44	F/O Didier **SCUVIE**	RAF No. 143484	(BEL)/RAF	**AA853**	MN-C	†
	W/O Guy **DE JAEGHER**	RAF No. 1299828	(BEL)/RAF	**AR498**	MN-G	
06.06.44	F/L François **VENESOEN**	RAF No. 107235	(BEL)/RAF	**EN950**	MN-H	†
08.06.44	F/O Albert **HERREMAN**	RAF No. 146066	(BEL)/RAF	**BM363**	MN-G	†
10.06.44	P/O Robert **ALEXANDRE**	RAF No. 134055	(BEL)/RAF	**AA720**	MN-J	†
	F/O Peter A. **WILSON**	RAF No. 153041	RAF	**BM422**	MN-P	†
14.06.44	F/O Lucien **LELARGE**	RAF No. 127854	(BEL)/RAF	**EE723**	MN-F	-

01.09.44	*Destroyed by V-1 on the ground*	-	-	**RM695**	MN-S	-
25.10.44	F/Sgt Ludovic **LAMBRECHTS**	RAF No. 1899871	(BEL)/RAF	**RM615**		-
04.11.44	S/L Léopold **COLLIGNON**	RAF No. 116288	(BEL)/RAF	**NH716**	MN-X	-
14.11.44	F/O Ferdinand **VERPOORTEN**	RAF No. 169600	(BEL)/RAF	**RM671**		-
08.12.44	F/Sgt Robert **JAMINÉ**	RAF No. 1424883	(BEL)/RAF	**RB145**		-
18.12.44	F/L Roger **HOORNAERT**	RAF No. 128392	(BEL)/RAF	**RM691**	MN-Q	-
24.12.44	S/L Léopold **COLLIGNON**	RAF No. 116288	(BEL)/RAF	**RM690**		**Inj.**
25.12.44	F/O Jacob **VANDERPERREN**	RAF No. 120896	(BEL)/RAF	**RM673**	MN-K	†
01.01.45	*Destroyed in air raid*	-	-	**RM622**		-
16.01.45	F/L Herman **SMETS**	RAF No. 87694	(BEL)/RAF	**RM619**	MN-D	**PoW**
23.01.45	F/Sgt Robert **HUENS**	RAF No. 1899804	(BEL)/RAF	**NH711**		†
11.02.45	F/Sgt Joseph **LALOUX**	RAF No. 1299839	(BEL)/RAF	**NH685**		**PoW**
26.02.45	S/L Terence **SPENCER**	RAF No. 47269	RAF	**RM739**	MN-H	**Eva.**
04.04.45	F/L Roger **HOORNAERT**	RAF No. 128392	(BEL)/RAF	**RB183**	MN-Z	**PoW**
05.04.45	P/O Anthony **CRESSWELL-TURNER**	RAF No. 152668	RAF	**RB185**	MN-L	**PoW**
15.04.45	F/Sgt Jacob **VANLIEFLAND**	RAF No. 1424983	(BEL)/RAF	**SM830**		-
19.04.45	S/L Terence **SPENCER**	RAF No. 47269	RAF	**SM814**	MN-A	**PoW**
20.04.45	F/L Kenneth **SMITH**	RAF No. 115521	RAF	**RM744**	MN-L	**Eva.**
	F/Sgt Jacques **GROENSTEEN**	RAF No. 1299851	(BEL)/RAF	**NH686**	MN-V	†
24.04.45	F/L Guy DE **PATOUL**	RAF No. 87684	(BEL)/RAF	**RM618**	MN-P	**PoW**

Total: 57

[1] Executed during the 'Great Escape' of March 1944.

The Belgians of 350 Sqn paid a high price with three experienced pilots killed during the first days of the D-Day landings in June 1944. The first was Flight Lieutenant 'Sus' Venesoen on 6 June. Below left, P/O A. Herreman was under training when Belgium was overrun. He completed his training after being evacuated to England. In 1942 he was flying with 124 Sqn, equipped with the rare Spitfire VI at the time, and was the only Belgian pilot to make a claim flying this variant. He was posted to 350 in September 1942 and killed on 8 June 1944. Below and centre, P/O R. Alexandre was an observer with the *Aéronautique Militaire* in 1939. He was re-trained as a fighter pilot and was among the founding members of 350 in November 1941. He was serving as a flight commander when he was posted missing on 10 June. Others, like 'Roberto' Muls, had better luck. He received his nickname as he was born in Spain, his father working as a Belgian diplomat there. Incarcerated in June 1941, he was eventually deported in September and arrived in Britain via Glasgow in January 1942. Enlisting in June, and after having served with various second-line units, he eventually joined 350 in May 1944. He survived the war.
(André Bar)

Flight A (above) and Flight B (below) at the end of January 1943.
From left to right (A Flight): in the front row, F/Sgt J. Rigole, Sgt F. Verpoorten, F/Sgt F. Boute (†13.11.43), F/O R. Dehasse (†24.03.43 with 91 Sqn), F/O F. Venesoen (†06.06.44), F/L H.J. Smets (Flight CO - PoW 16.01.45) and F/O L.C. Collignon. On the wing, P/O L. Lelarge, Sgt G. de Jaegher, Sgt J. Groensteen (†20.04.45) and P/O R. Van de Poel (†11.07.43). On the engine is Sgt J. Van Lerberghe.
B Flight: P/O P. Siroux, F/O R. Alexandre (†10.06.44), F/L A. Plisnier (Flight CO), P/O A.E. Claesen (†07.01.45 - 349 Sqn), Sgt A.C. Michiels (†16.07.44 in a Miles Magister of the FTTC), F/O G. Deltour and F/O E.J. Plas (†28.03.43 - 610 Sqn). On the wing, Sgt J. Wustefeld, Sgt L.J. Harmel and Sgt J. Lavigne. On the engine is Sgt L. Verbeeck. 'Coco' Collignon left 350 soon after for 64 Sqn, but would become OC in October 1944 until being severely wounded in action on 24 December 1944. *(André Bar)*

Date	Pilot	S/N	Origin	Serial	Code	Fate
SPITFIRE Mk II						
24.11.41	Sgt Antoon E.L. **CLAESEN**	RAF No. 1299923	(BEL)/RAF	**P8661***	MN-U	**Inj.**
09.01.42	F/L Jacques A. **CARLIER**	RAF No. 87701	(BEL)/RAF	**P8702**	MN-Z	-
SPITFIRE Mk V						
17.02.42	F/Sgt Henri **LIMET**	RAF No. 1299911	(BEL)/RAF	**W3525**	MN-V	-
12.04.42	Sgt José **HANSEZ**	RAF No. 1299901	(BEL)/RAF	**AD472**	MN-P	-
11.07.43	F/O Raymond **VAN DE POEL**	RAF No. 100999	(BEL)/RAF	**EN860**	MN-B	†
	Sgt Marcel **GRAWELS**	RAF No. 1299842	(BEL)/RAF	**BM399**	MN-W	†
21.03.44	Sgt Mathieu **MOREL**	RAF No. 1424812	(BEL)/RAF	**AB931**	MN-T	-
29.03.44	F/O Guy **BECKERS**	RAF No. 117602	(BEL)/RAF	**EN854**	MN-H	-
SPITFIRE Mk IX						
08.07.44	Sgt Joseph F. **WOOLEY**	RAF No. 1578305	RAF	**MK123**		†
13.07.44	F/O Paul **DELORME**	RAF No. 157939	(BEL)/RAF	**MK301**		-
SPITFIRE Mk XIV						
27.08.44	F/Sgt Joseph **LALOUX**	RAF No. 1299839	(BEL)/RAF	**RM751**	MN-T	-
11.11.44	F/Sgt Mathieu **MOREL**	RAF No. 1424812	(BEL)/RAF	**RB168**	MN-X	†
09.06.45	F/O Guy **DE BUEGER**	RAF No. 130772	(BEL)/RAF	**RM869**	MN-V	-
17.12.45	F/Sgt Gaston **DE GERLACHE DE G.**	RAF No. 1814881	(BEL)/RAF	**NH660**	MN-S	-
SPITFIRE Mk XVI						
05.10.46	W/C Léon **PRÉVOT**	RAF No. 84285	(BEL)/RAF	**TB124**		-

Total: 15

*Spitfire Mk IIB

A scene of 350 Sqn on 12 February 1942 as the unit is prepared for a parade. Only one Spitfire can be identified in this photo – P7810/MN-D, recently taken on charge, replaced P8020 which had used the same individual code. This letter was assumed by P8147 following the eventual departure of P7810 from the squadron. In January and February 1942, a part turnover of airframes on hand occurred and the following Spitfire IIs were received: P7376, P7543, P7620/O, P7744/N, P7810, P8089, P8147/D, P8200/T and P8141/K. *(André Bar)*

Various scenes of 350 Sqn while it was part of the occupying forces in Germany. Above, some Spitfire XIVs lined-up and, below, Spitfire XIV MN-Z (probably RB180) parked behind a captured Fieseler 156. These photos were taken at Fassberg during the summer of 1945. *(André Bar)*

Spitfire MV267 was issued to 350 Sqn in mid-June 1945. It was part of the last batch with the new canopy and carried the two 0.50-in machine gun armament. Below, Spitfire RN198/MN-T, received in July 1945, with the classic canopy.
(André Bar)

In August 1946, 350 was re-equipped with Spitfire Mk XVIs as 349, part of the same wing, was already equipped with the type. At the time the Belgians had been authorised to use the Belgian roundels on their aircraft. Above TB252/MN-J below, three Spitfires seen parked at Fassberg, TD281/MN-S being in the forefront, TB137/MN-K on its right.
(André Bar)

Victories - confirmed or probable claims: 6.0 + 1 V-1

First operational sortie:
27.08.43
Last operational sortie:
04.05.45

Number of sorties: *ca.* 4,300

Total aircraft written-off: 47

Aircraft lost on operations: 32
Aircraft lost in accidents: 15

Squadron code letters:
GE

COMMANDING OFFICERS

S/L Roger MALENGREAU	RAF No. 82160	(BEL)/RAF	09.01.43	08.06.43
S/L Yvan DU MONCEAU DE B.	RAF No. 87700	(BEL)/RAF	08.06.43	21.07.44
S/L Albert VAN DE VELDE	RAF No. 123067	(BEL)/RAF	21.07.44	31.03.45
S/L Raymond LALLEMAND*	RAF No. 116472	(BEL)/RAF	31.03.45	17.12.45
S/L Albert VAN DE VELDE	RAF No. 123067	(BEL)/RAF	17.12.45	24.10.46

posted non-effective sick from 02.10.45 onwards

SQUADRON USAGE

Number 349 Squadron was the second and last Belgian squadron to be formed in the RAF. It was first formed in West Africa on 9 January 1943 for air defense duty, but after two months of intensive training on Tomahawks, the pilots were finally used to ferry aircraft, the defense of the area being seen as not a priority after all. Most of the pilots were not Belgians and during this phase a few accidents were reported and the most important took place on 12 March 1943 when P/O MacDonald, in Tomahawk AH859, force-landed in the bush, 2 miles East of Ikeja. The accident was due to engine failure, the machine being a complete write-off. The pilot had a miraculous escape, freeing himself from the burning aircraft and walking to the Officer's Mess whence he was rushed to the 68th General Hospital. He was found to be suffering from a compound fracture of the cheek-bone, a badly

Roger Malengreau enlisted in the Belgian Army in 1936 to become a pilot. In May 1940 he was an Army Cooperation pilot flying Fairey Foxes when Belgium was invaded by the Germans. Within two days his unit lost all of its aircraft and the personnel escaped to France. Continuing his retreat in France, despite the fact that Belgium had surrendered, Malengreau did not return to his country but sailed to the UK instead after France signed the Armistice at the end of June 1940. Arriving in England on 9 July, he enlisted in the RAF and was re-trained as a fighter pilot and, upon completion of his training, was posted to No. 87 Squadron in August. He was one of the 29 Belgians to participate in the Battle of Britain. In December he was posted to No. 56 Squadron, then to No. 609 Squadron and opened his score on 30 June 1941, sharing the probable destruction of a Bf109 and adding another probable on 14 July. In October 1942 he was posted to No. 171 Squadron but in November he was offered the position of CO of the second Belgian fighter unit, No. 349 (Belgian) Squadron, then based in Nigeria in Western Africa. He accepted this posting and officially took over on 1 January 1943. At his own request, the squadron, which was intended to serve in the Belgian Congo, was eventually repatriated to the UK, where it was thought it would be more useful, and he left 349 upon arrival back in England. No more operational postings followed before the end of war and he left the military after the war and began a career in the Belgian Foreign Service.
(André Bar)

Ikeja, March 1943: Most of the officers are British but the Belgians are:
Front row: F/L C. Roman (3rd from left), the OC S/L R. Malengreau (centre), F/O A. Vanderbranden (1st from right)
Middle row: F/O O. Lejeune (2nd from right), F/O A. Drossaert (1st from right)
Back row: F/O R. Demoulin (2nd from right, †06.04.44), P/O A. Lemaire (1st from right)

Below, a Tomahawk being prepared a the ferry fight. Front left F/Sgt H. Goblet (Belgian). He followed 349 in the UK and later served with the Belgian flight of 609 Squadron. He was shot down and became a PoW on 3 March 1945. On the front right, W/O G. Bouriano, a Belgian chief mechanic.
(André Bar)

sprained ankle and minor cuts. In April, 349 began to ferry Kittyhawks Mk II and sadly one British F/Sgt E. Orbrart pilot of the squadron was killed on the 9th in Chad. The same month, 349 had to deplore the death of F/L R. Wilmot who died from natural causes on the 28th, a former 609 Sqn pilot. By that time 349's role to defend the area and ferry aircraft, when Axis troops were about to surrender, was not justified anymore. When the surrender came into effect in May, it was felt that 349 would be more useful in England. Therefore, it was disbanded and reformed on 5 June 1943 at Wittering, east of Leicester, on the Spitfire Mk.V. It moved almost immediately to nearby Collyweston. Command was given to S/L I. du Monceau de Bergendael , a very experienced pilot who had been serving as a flying instructor with 61 OTU after a successful tour with 350 Squadron. He would lead the unit throughout its time on the Spitfire Mk.V.

The first few weeks were spent organising the arrival of pilots and machines. The first Spitfire test flight took place on the 24th. At the end of the month, a second move was made to Kingscliffe, south of Wittering. In July, the overseas element joined 349, as the unit continued training, and the full complement of aircraft was achieved. On 25 July, the first major incident occurred when, while practicing a dive, P/O M. Balasse lost control of his aircraft. He was thrown out of the cockpit and severely injured when his parachute opened at a very low altitude. The Spitfire was destroyed in the ensuing crash. In August, the squadron made three more moves: Wellingore on the 5th, Digby on the 16th, and, eventually, Acklington, north of Newcastle, on the 25th. The squadron was considered operational, but the area was not the best for encounters with the Luftwaffe. However, on 27 August, F/L A. Van der Velve, the A Flight CO, and F/O A. Van Hecke, who were on readiness, were scrambled to intercept an unidentified aircraft, but it turned out to be a Mosquito. September was quiet, but, from the 6th, A Flight was detached to Digby. At Acklington, if the convoy patrol performed by F/L G. Seydel, the B Flight CO, and F/O A. Lemaire on the 15th is ignored, nothing of interest happened as the time was spent training and participating in several co-operation exercises. In October, 349 was notified that it would be equipped with the Spitfire LF.V for long range and low altitude ops. On 12 October, the squadron suffered its first loss when F/O A. Van Hecke was killed when caught by bad weather while trying to get to the aerodrome. This loss occurred a couple of days before the move to Friston, near Brighton on the coast, a move that indicated 349 would now be engaged over the Continent. After their arrival on the 22nd, the squadron wasted no time in getting back on operations and, two days later, S/L de Monceau de Bergendael led the squadron on an uneventful Ramrod to escort bombers targeting Beauvais-Tillé aerodrome in France. On 26 October, the squadron moved to Southend for an Air Firing Course, returning to Friston on the 10th. The next day, a second sweep was carried out in the middle of the afternoon, an escort for Mitchells heading to Audinghen. This was also uneventful. Bad weather hampered the next two escorts on the 12th and 13th. The following few days were reserved for various training sorties and the next op took place on the 19th with the squadron's involvement in an escort of American Marauders attacking Saint-André airfield. The weather was responsible for the cancellation of further operations but, at the end of November, the squadron was able to complete six escorts in three

Spitfire AA751/GE-K being serviced at Friston. This Spitfire was issued to 349 at the end of October 1943. It remained on strength until the unit converted to the Mk.IX. At the end of February 1944, the other Spitfire Vs on charge were W3373/X, AA765/I, AA944, AD238, AR292/T, AR293/Y, AR328/M, AR437/J, AL334/F, BL385/O, BL630, BL642/C, EE660/Z, EE745/V, EP509/R and EP660/Q. *(André Bar)*

Spitfire EP354/GE-L at dispersal in January 1944. (*André Bar*)

days. Indeed, the Allies had to take advantage of any good day to achieve their goals as they had started to increase pressure on various targets as the build up to the invasion of Europe continued. The squadron was airborne on the 23rd, 25th and 26th. Excluding some early returns due to mechanical trouble, all taskings were uneventful. November closed with a scramble on the 30th by F/O J. Ester and Sgt J. Van Molkot to try to locate a friendly bomber in distress. They found a severely damaged Flying Fortress well out over the Channel and helped the American pilot return to England. The weather improved a little in December, allowing the Belgians to fly more often. That said, only ten days proved clear enough and, in all, the squadron logged 139 sorties in December. The New Year brought nothing different as far as the operations were concerned. The squadron was still involved in bomber escorts over the Continent. While the weather didn't improve that much in January 1944, the Belgians were able to get airborne for almost half of the month. Therefore, the number of sorties increased to 165. However, 349 mourned its first operational loss on the 2nd. That afternoon, four Spitfires led by F/L A. Van de Velde went out on a Rhubarb. They did not locate the target, but, on the return leg, they were intercepted by four Fw190s. The Belgians engaged, but could not get into a good position to shoot at any of them. Furthermore, F/L Van de Velde soon had his windscreen covered in oil. When both sides disengaged, Van de Velde called his men on the radio and all replied that they were okay. However, while Van der Velde, P/O H. Bailly and Sgt A. Moureau landed back at base, F/Sgt A. Van den Broeck was not seen again. The rest of the month was rather uneventful and looked like it would close on that note when, on the 31st at around 4.00 pm, F/Sgt H. Limet experienced an engine failure and fire during an air test. He was fortunately able to escape from his aircraft and landed almost unscathed. With regard to sorties flown, the squadron did not do any better with just 162 completed. The first eight ops, which took place between the 3rd and the 10th, were completed without major incident. However, 11 February would be different. That day, at 14.35, nine Spitfires took for *Ramrod* 545 to escort eighteen Mosquitos, flying in two boxes of six and twelve aircraft, on a low-level bombing raid, the main target being V-1 launchers at Fréval. The op started badly with the engine of the Spitfire flown by F/O J. Fromont giving trouble just after take off. Fromont decided to return base immediately, but the engine died before he could do so. The Spitfire crashed and, while the pilot escaped unhurt, was a total write-off. In the meantime, the eight remaining aircraft continued their escort and crossed the French coast. Not far from Épinay, while the Mosquitos were over the target, P/O J. Croquet was seen to crash near the town. He had been hit in the engine by flak, thick white smoke pouring from the exhaust, and had no choice but to force his Spitfire down even though he considered ditching into the Channel in the hope of being rescued. Shocked by the rough landing, he was rescued by French civilians. He was hidden and was finally liberated the following August. He rejoined 349 in September. His compatriots, however, were facing a run of bad luck as the following day another Spitfire was wrecked when F/L Van der Velde (A Flight CO) crashed on take off for a test flight. He managed to stop the Spitfire crashing into a parked aircraft (AR432). When taken to hospital, it was found that he had a broken back and would be off flying for some time. He was replaced at the head of the flight by F/L A. Drossaert. These losses were sustained as 349 was about to receive the Spitfire IX, the process beginning five days later on the 17th. During this interim period,

Yvan du MONCEAU DE BERGENDAEL
RAF No. 87700

'Duke' Du Monceau attended the Belgian Royal Military Academy and was posted to a cavalry unit as a lieutenant in 1938. The following year he was transferred to the *Aéronautique Militaire* and was still under training when Belgium was invaded. The school was evacuated and he eventually reached the UK via Morocco in July 1940. He enlisted in the RAF, completed his training and was posted in April 1941 to No. 253 Squadron, then to No. 56 Squadron, and finally to No. 609 (West Riding) Squadron to fly Spitfires. He remained with 609 for almost a year, but during that lapse of time he made eight claims, the first, a damaged Bf109, on 3 July 1941. At the end of March 1942 he was posted to No. 350 (Belgian) Squadron as a flight commander and received the DFC in July. More successes were filed in 1942 and on 12 December he made his final claim with a destroyed Fw190. His score had risen to eight confirmed, three probables and six damaged. He was posted out for a rest a couple of days later. In June 1943 he returned for a second tour of operations as OC No. 349 (Belgian) Squadron. He led the unit until July 1944 and was awarded a Bar to his DFC. Until the end of the war he served in various staff positions and did not return to operational duty. He continued to serve with the new Belgian Air Force after the war and had reached the rank of Major-General by the time of his retirement in January 1972.

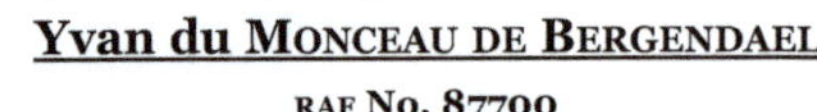

Supermarine Spitfire Mk.VB BL540
No. 350 (Belgian) Squadron
Flight Lieutenant Y. du Monceau de Bergendael
Atcham (UK), April 1942

Supermarine Spitfire Mk.IX ML365
No. 349 (Belgian) Squadron
Squadron Leader Y. du Monceau de Bergendael
Selsey (UK), June 1944

the squadron continued to fly its Spitfire Vs and their last op was carried out on the 22nd when four aircraft led by F/L Drossaert participated in an escort of 72 Marauders attacking Gilze-Rijen airfield.

The conversion was coupled with a transfer from Air Defence of Great Britain to 83 Group of 2TAF, meaning much more action could be expected. The Mk.IXs were received in mid-February and conversion proceeded easily. The first on Mk.IXs on 25 February. *Ramrod* 589 was an uneventful escort for fourteen Mosquitos attacking a target near Belleville in Normandy. A Ranger was flown the next day, followed by another escort on the 29th (*Ramrod* 601), but, again, these proved uneventful. By the end of the month, 349 was operating MH610/Z, MJ294/X, MJ353/J, MJ369/H, MJ569/L, MJ748/A, MJ879/G, MJ889/W MJ962/F, MJ964/T, MK130/P, MK135/K, MK136/N, MK148/R, MK153/S, MK175/B, MK233/C, MK354/V and MK363/U. Little operational flying was performed in March, with only five days contributing sixty sorties. More importantly, the squadron moved to Hornchurch on the 11th. Early April was quiet, no ops were flown, but intensive training focussed on dive-bombing. The squadron moved to Selsey, near Portsmouth, on 11 April. The first days at Selsey were plagued by various accidents, with one crash, on the 13th, seriously damaging the Spitfire and another, following a technical failure two days later at Westhampnett, wrote off the aircraft. The pilot, F/Sgt R. Vanderbosh escaped without injury. Operations resumed on the 18th after several cancellations due to bad weather. The op involved dive-bombing a target near Abbeville with the Wing; good results were obtained. The squadron went on air cover beyond Dieppe on the 20th and followed up with a fighter sweep beyond Saint-Omer. Both were uneventful. The next day 349 returned to the Abbeville area for another dive-bombing attack. While some good results were again confirmed, the flak was accurate and F/O J. Moreau de Melen was hit in the engine. He managed to get his aircraft over the Channel, baled out twenty miles off Beachy Head, and, fortunately, was picked up by a Walrus within forty minutes. The squadron was airborne almost every day for the rest of the month, but further operational losses were sustained. On the 28th, while escorting American Marauders, F/Sgt H. Limet did not switch to the main tank before his extra tanks ran dry (probably caused by an air lock in his fuel system) and made a forced landing near the Seine river. He was taken prisoner. The next day, F/Sgt A. Moureau crashed on taking-off from Friston while returning to Selsey. He escaped injury, but his Spitfire was only good for parts salvage. In May, as the weather permitted flying without restriction, about 350 escort and dive-bombing sorties, sometimes flown from Manston, were carried out. On the 9th, the wing leader, W/C P.J. Simpson, flew with the squadron while the Wing escorted bombers attacking the Abbeville marshalling yards. No incident was reported. This was not the case the day after. During another bomber escort, targeting the Creil marshalling yards this time, F/O P. Libert experienced engine trouble and had to bale out. May 10 was not a lucky day for him as, exactly four years previously, he was badly burnt when a German bomb set fire to his Hurricane at Schaeffen in Belgium. This time the consequences were different as he was immediately taken prisoner. Despite intensive flying, no further losses were recorded until the 21st when, while attacking a ground target, F/O M. Sans was hit by flak. He managed to keep control of his machine despite the huge hole in the right wing. When he had Beachy Head in sight, and with control of the Spitfire becoming increasingly difficult, he elected to bale out over the Channel. Fortunately, he was picked up half an hour later. The same misadventure happened to F/O J. Ester,

Spitfire MJ294 was among the first Mk.IXs taken on charge in February 1944. This aircraft became the first Mk.IX flown by S/L du Monceau. *(André Bar)*

No. 349 Squadron did its Air Firing Practice at Ayr in Scotland in intensely cold weather. Above, MK175/GE-B and below, MK148/GE-R. *(André Bar)*

Pilots of 349 Sqn at Selsey in March 1944:
Left to right, back row: Flight Sergeants G. Halleux, J. Gheyssens (†08.06.44), J. Van Molkot, H. Limet, A. Moureau, and J. Moureau, F/O Ph. Maskens, P/O H. Goldsmit (†03.11.44), and Dr. J. Degand MO.
Second row: Cpl Barnes (groundcrew - British), F/Sgt J. Groensteen (†20.04.45 with 350), Flying Officers A. Lemaire, J. Fromont, M. Siraut, P. Libert, M. Sans (†07.06.44), and J. Moreau, Sgt L. Vingerhoets (groundcrew - Belgian), and Cpl Howe (groundcrew - British).
Front row: Cpl E. Dickson (groundcrew - British), Flight Lieutenants H.W. Gulson (A&SD - British), and A. Drossaert, CO Y. du Monceau, Flight Lieutenants G. Seydel and E. Piercot, and Sgt Innes (groundcrew - British).
(André Bar)

who baled out ten miles off Le Tréport, but he had to spend an hour and a half in the water before being rescued by a Walrus that then developed a leak and nearly sank on the spot. Another Walrus eventually came to the rescue. Operations continued as usual in to June until D-Day and all went well. On 6 June, the pilots woke up very early and were at readiness from 04.40. The first sortie was carried out at 05.30 with a patrol on the eastern flank of the invading forces. No enemy aircraft were seen on this sortie or the second one which took place mid-morning. A third patrol, led by F/L G. Seydel, was flown in the middle of the afternoon. A few miles north-east of Caen, F/O J. Moreau de Melen saw a Ju88 diving westward from cloud three miles south-west of Cabourg. He immediately jettisoned his bomb and went after this Ju88 with his number two, F/Sgt J. Moureau. The Germans saw the two Spitfires approaching and the pilot dived to zero feet along the canal running north-east of Caen. Moreau followed in line astern, firing an ineffectual burst with cannon and machine guns from 600 yards. At the same time F/Sgt Moureau fired a short machine gun burst. The chase continued and F/O Moreau managed to open fire again with two second bursts, seeing strikes on the fuselage. The Junkers continued on and changed direction to head west again. Moreau closed in and fired a four second burst with all of his weapons, closing from 250 yards to 200 yards. Many strikes were seen on the right engine and forward part of the fuselage. A cowling and many pieces flew away, but the Junkers was still airborne and now Moreau was out of ammunition. Flight Sergeant Moureau closed in now and, from a good position, fired a two second burst with cannons and machine guns, closing from 200 to 150 yards, and hit the Junkers in the fuselage and cockpit. The Ju88 now appeared to be fatally hit as it climbed out of control to the right. Moureau followed and fired a final burst of three seconds from 30°. He broke away as the Junkers dived to the ground where it exploded ten miles west of Caen. The victory was shared by the two Belgian pilots. This Ju88 was not the only encounter as others were attacked by 349 pilots, adding further claims to the squadron's ledger. The destruction of another Ju88 was shared by two other Belgian pilots, F/Sgt J. van Melkot and Sgt J. Bragard, while four more were damaged. These were the first claims credited to 349. Flight Sergeant van Melkot did not have time to celebrate his claim, however, as, while heading for home, he received a direct flak hit in the engine. He immediately turned back towards the Allied lines but the engine stopped about thirty seconds later, smoke and flames coming out of the spinner and cowling. He made a crash-landing east of Colombelles and was eventually taken prisoner. He was released by US troops near Rennes on 4 August but never flew on operations again. Later that day a fourth sortie was carried out but proved uneventful. The next day, the 7th, started well for 349 as F/L G. Seydel managed to engage a Fw190 south-west of Caen as it diced with two other Spitfires near the town; he lodged a damaged claim as a result. Sadly, that claim was overshadowed during the following patrol of the day when F/O M. Sans was killed after being shot down by flak near Carpiquet. The next day also produced mixed results. Patrols continued over the landing beaches and, on the first one, at 06.25, Seydel, who was leading, saw some Fw190s flying eastwards and jettisoning their bombs over the sea about six miles west of Trouville. He made a 360° turn and dived to 500 feet where he found himself just behind the last Fw190 as the other pilots of the patrol took up the

Scenes at Selsey in February-March 1944. Above, Spitfire MJ748/GE-A having its left 20mm cannon cleaned. This aircraft has the squadron emblem painted under the exhausts, but this practice was very short-lived and not all of the Spitfires received this decoration.
Below, in the background, MK354/GE-V and, on its right, MK148/GE-R being prepared for their next flight. MJ354 was initially regularly flown by F/O J. Moreau.
(André Bar)

chase. He fired a short burst with cannons, closing from 700 to 500 yards, whereupon the Fw190 made a climbing turn to the left. He closed in again and fired two short bursts with cannons and machine guns from 200 yards, seeing strikes on the left wing and fuselage. The hood blew off and pieces fell away from the aircraft. Just behind, his number two, W/O D. Clarke, a Kiwi, had followed and began to fire at the Fw190 as well so Seydel broke away. The Fw190 was seen to dive and explode on impact with the ground. The victory was shared by the two pilots. The presence of Clarke, and several other Commonwealth flyers, was due to a temporary shortage of operational Belgian pilots. In the meantime, the other Fw190s had been engaged but the advantage swung to the Germans who managed to shoot down F/Sgt J. Gheyssens who was seen to bale out west of Dinan-sur-Mer. He did not survive and was killed the day of his 28 years old. During the following patrol, Fw190s were again encountered, but the German aircraft rapidly flew out of range. The third patrol of the day proved uneventful. Intensive flying occurred over the next few days but, even though the Luftwaffe remained very active in the area, nothing more than furtive encounters were recorded as far as 349 was concerned. The squadron suffered some more losses though. On the 12th, upon returning to base from a patrol, F/Sgt R. Vandenbosch collided with the Spitfire of F/O A. Oger who, after trying to follow F/O J. Fromont all over the sky over the bridgehead, had stopped short of petrol just off the runway. The rest of the month remained intense and, by its end, more than 630 sorties had been logged. The squadron then moved with the Wing to Coolham. This stay was brief as another move was made to Funtington, near Chichester, on 4 July. The moves hampered the operational tempo with 475 sorties flown for the month. The new move came with a new role: escorting Bomber Command heavy bombers or 2TAF medium bombers. Some sweeps or standing patrols were also occasionally flown. Despite this high number of sorties, no operational losses were recorded that month even though, on the 12th, a recently posted in British pilot, F/O A.A.G. Patiny, was killed in a flying accident near Biggin Hill. He apparently failed to recover from a 45° dive for unknown reasons. A few days later a change of command took place, S/L du Monceau being at the end of his tour, with the A Flight commander, F/L A. Van de Velde, taking charge. Further changes occurred at the same time as the B Flight commander, G. Seydel, was also tour expired. The two newly promoted Flight COs were Flying Officers L. Lelarge and P. Siroux, both ex-350, who would arrive in due course. A few days later, the 26th, despite July being relatively uneventful from an operational point of view, 349 scored against the Luftwaffe. That day, 135 Wing was tasked with escorting 36 Mitchells and 24 Bostons from 2TAF to attack a dump at Alençon. About thirty German fighters tried to intercept, but the Spitfires were ready for them. The Belgians were the ones who scored the most and two confirmed victories were filed. One went to F/L Siroux and the second was claimed by F/L Seydel who was flying his final ops with 349. The latter got a Bf109 at 18,000 feet with two bursts, the first a half a second burst of cannons and machine guns from dead astern and above. He saw hits in the cockpit and right wing root before the Bf109 turned slowly on its back and went down in a vertical dive. Seydel followed the fatally damaged fighter and fired another burst of two

Soon after D-Day, S/L du Monceau began to regularly fly a new Spitfire IX (ML365). The letter 'I' painted on the D-Day stripes suggests the aircraft was coded GE-I, possibly referring to his first name, Ivan, the English variant of Yvan. *(André Bar)*

Carpiquet, Normandy, end of summer 1944. Left to right: F/Sgt J. Leroy (PoW 22.01.45), possibly F/O J. Wood (British), possibly F/Sgt N. Leroy (J. Leroy's brother), P/O G. Halleux, F/Sgt J. Bragard, unknown, P/O A. Oger, F/Sgt A. Moureau, P/O R. Vandenbosch, S/L van de Velde, unknown, and F/O P. Erkes walking in front of Spitfire Mk IX PT385/GE-T.
Jean and Norbert Leroy were students in May 1940 who managed to flee Belgium for the USA where their parents were living. Later on, in January 1942, they both went to Canada to enlist in the RAF. They eventually joined together 349 Sqn in August 1944. Both survived the war, but Jean as a PoW. *(André Bar)*

seconds from 300 yards, seeing pieces fly away. Flight Lieutenant Seydel started to orbit and observed the Bf109 going down vertically and hitting the ground at the corner of a wood where it burst into flames. Three other pilots made claims: F/Sgt D.A. Smerdon (British), F/O A. Uydens and F/O J. Ester each claimed a damaged Bf109. No loss was recorded by the Belgians. What they did not know, however, was that these were the last claims of the war credited to the squadron; at least against aircraft as, two days later, F/O J. Moreau, returning from a bomber escort attacking Noball sites west of Lille, sighted a V-1 and shot it down north of Tonbridge.

An unusual event took place during the first week of August. On the evening of the 4th, a V-1 bomb crashed in B Flight's dispersal after a Mosquito tipped it over with its wings. The bomb started to burn less than fifteen yards from a Spitfire with full tanks. The mechanics dragged it to safety but the aircraft was a total write-off from the blast. Surprisingly, despite some minor damage to another Spitfire, only one person was slightly injured. During this first week 349 flew its ops as usual but, two days after the V-1 incident, it moved back to Selsey where ops remained unchanged, escorts with some sweeps between two Ramrods. On 18 August the squadron operated from the continent for the first time, carrying out two sweeps from B.10 before returning home. The unit moved again on 20 August, this time to Tangmere. It stayed there less than a week while preparing to move to the continent on the 30th after a couple of postponements. The ground party was flown to B.17/Caen-Carpiquet as early as 26 August. In the meantime, the pilots continued to operate from Tangmere. Sadly, on the 30th, while on a sweep over the Scheldt-Lys area south of Gant, ground targets were strafed and F/O M. Renard posted missing. He was last heard saying he was heading home and that his engine was over-heating. While he was unable to reach Allied lines, he managed to evade capture. The next day, 349 began its operations from France for 2TAF. From then on, the nature of the squadron's tasks changed, focusing on Army support. The stay at Carpiquet was short as, to follow the rapid Allied advance, another move was made on 8 September, the new location being B.35/Le Tréport, then B.53/Merville on the 12th. Merville was home for the Belgians for the next six weeks. In September 349 flew more than 300 sorties but, while many ground targets were attacked and mostly destroyed, luck was with the squadron as no losses were suffered. In October, despite the autumnal weather gradually taking hold, 349 managed to log 340 sorties, claiming numerous targets destroyed or damaged on the ground. This time, however, the squadron sustained some losses. The first two occurred within two days. Flying Officer A. Vanderheyden was hit by flak near Gouda while attacking ground targets on the 5th. He was initially heard asking for a course home and later to say he was baling out; he evaded capture with the help of Dutch civilians and was back home on 22 October. The next day, while carrying out the second armed recce, this time near Amersfoort area in the Netherlands, some barges and METs were found and strafed, but W/O K.R. Brant (British) was hit by flak. He performed an emergency landing and initially

Albert VAN DE VELDE
RAF No. 123067

Albert Van de Velde joined the Belgian *Aéronautique Militaire* as an NCO in March 1936. In 1939 he was serving as an officer pilot flying the Fairey Fox, a reconnaissance biplane. His unit retreated to France and, after the Belgian surrender, he briefly stayed in France before returning to his country where he became a prisoner of war in August 1940. He was detained pending his transfer to Germany. Before that happened, he managed to escape in October and, in January 1941, left Belgium for the UK. He was successively interned in France and Spain, but reached Gibraltar in December. In March 1942 he enlisted in the RAF and was retrained. In October he attended 58 OTU before being posted to No. 91 (Nigeria) Squadron in January 1943. In June he was posted to No. 349 (Belgian) Squadron upon its formation, soon taking on a flight commander role. On 12 February 1944 he was badly injured while testing a Spitfire. Hospitalised, his injuries kept him away from the squadron until the end of April. He participated in the liberation of Europe with the squadron and made his only claim, a Ju88 damaged, on D-Day. He eventually assumed command of 349 at the end of July 1944 and led it until tour-expired at the end of March 1945. The following month, he was awarded the DFC. He later returned to 349 to command before the squadron was transferred to the Belgian Air Force. He served with the Belgian Air Force until July 1960.

Supermarine Spitfire Mk. XVI TB900
No. 349 (Belgian) Squadron
Squadron Leader A. Van de Velde
B.152/Fassberg (Germany), spring 1946

evaded capture but was later taken prisoner west of Arnhem. Before Vanderheyden returned, the squadron experienced a very bad day on the 19th. In the morning support op, attacking the fort at Breskens, P/O C. de St-Aubin was lost to flak. On the return flight, his squadronmates heard him report over the radio that his oil pressure was zero, probably due to flak or gunfire damage. He tried to reach the Allied lines but had to fly low (about 1500 feet) and slow if he wanted to succeed. It was not enough. A few metres from the border of Belgium he crashed to his death in a field on the Zandstraat, probably after stalling too low to recover. In the afternoon, at approximately 16.00, S/L Van der Velde called on the R/T to say he had been hit by flak and was going down. From the little conversation that went on, he was unhurt and the pilots reported he was seen to land and get out of his aircraft. The CO was lucky as he crashed 200-300 yards from the front line defended by the Nova Scotia Highlanders of the Canadian Army. About a dozen soldiers came up to him and wanted to know why the aircraft was not marked with the usual black and white stripes on the wing. Van der Velde was able to convince them of his identity and was conveyed to the Battalion HQ time for tea. He was back with the squadron the next day. After a series of delays since 21 October, 349 moved to B.65/Maldeghem. The squadron operated from that base for the next two and a half months. The early days at Maldeghem were far from good, however, as the following day, after 349 dispatched aircraft in pairs to carry out armed recces in the Rheindahlen area, two pilots were posted missing – F/O H. Goldsmit and F/Sgt P. Decroix. Both were hit by flak when they entered a flak trap and both made an emergency landing. Decroix was later taken prisoner, but Goldsmit, who came down not far from the lines, managed to return. A few days later, on the 8th, another Spitfire was lost to flak while attacking ground targets near Dortrech. Flying Officer A. Uydens was hit over the target and was heard over the R/T to say his windscreen was damaged, but the engine still seemed to be running well and that he would make for base. The situation changed when he saw the coolant temperature rising rapidly and four minutes later reported he was crash landing within the Allied lines. He was seen to make a heavy landing; the aircraft turned over and one wing broke off. Flying Officer J. Croquet and F/Sgt J. Bragard stayed ten minutes, but Uydens was not seen to get out of the aircraft. Several civilians were seen in the vicinity and helped him get out before he was taken to a Canadian hospital. On 19 November, 349 only carried out one op to destroy a bridge and railway line near Amersfoort. The attack produced mixed results as, while the railway was cut, the bridge received no direct hits. Flak was as accurate as ever and hit the Spitfire flown by F/O M. Gendebien who was killed in the subsequent crash. Ten days later, Sgt R. Van Wymers was shot down and killed while attacking a German HQ near Dunkirk. November was a stand-out month for two reasons, neither of them positive; it was the most costly month with five Spitfire lost, two pilots killed and one taken PoW, and just 220 sorties were flown, the lowest total since D-Day. December reversed the trend with more than 280 sorties flown and only one loss reported (F/O M. Renard was killed on the 25th). Sent with eight other aircraft for a sweep near Saint-Vith for the second show of the day, Renard was seen returning from the attack, indicating a mechanical problem, and pointed downwards suggesting he was going to land. Sadly, he was killed in the crash.

Maldegem airfield was attacked by the Luftwaffe at around 09.20 on 1 January 1945 during Operation *Bodenplatte*. Considerable losses of aircraft were reported, but 349 was lucky and only one Spitfire was destroyed on the ground. The disturbance didn't last too long as 349 was airborne before midday for an armed recce on the Breda-Hertogenbosch road area. Armed recces were carried out as far as the weather permitted and about 180 were flown in January. A few major incidents were experienced, first on the 5th when F/O A. Vandenheyden and P/O R. Vandenbosch were forced to land after an attack on suspected German troop accommodation. Four more Spitfires were also hit, a good result considering this strongpoint was defended with effective small arms.

Spitfire Mk IX PT891/GE-E taxiing from B.53/Melville with a 500-lb bomb under its belly. *(André Bar)*

Spitfire IX RK809/GE-V at B.77/Gilze-Rijen in February 1945 just before 349 left for Predannack in England. *(André Bar)*

Vandenbosch was forced to crash land between Geertruidenberg and Raamsdonksveer. His number two circled the crash site and waited until the pilot had left his aircraft, waving his arms to indicate he was uninjured. His Spitfire was later recovered and repaired, while Vandenheyden landed at B.77 with oil pressure trouble and was soon back at base. These were the only major events before the squadron moved to B.77/Gilze-Rigen in Holland on the 13th. Operations continued as usual from the new base but, one week later, an attack on several trains resulted in the loss of F/Sgt J. Leroy who was possibly hit by flak. He was heard over the target area to say he had engine trouble and was turning for base. As this occurred well within the enemy lines, he did not make it, crashed on the German side and was reported missing. He was eventually taken prisoner. Another Spitfire was also damaged when, short of petrol, it crash-landed in a field in the Allied lines. The pilot, F/Sgt J. Branders, was uninjured and the aircraft repairable. With the weather improving, more sorties were carried out in February, with 180 flown in the first half of the month, the same amount flown for all of January. On 3 February, twelve aircraft took off for an armed recce over the Gorinchem area. From this operation F/Sgt L. van de Werve was lost when his section went down to attack a lorry. It was partially obscured by trees and the pilots overshot on the first run so the section came in again. When looking around, no one could see van de Werve, nor could he be contacted on the R/T, but debris of an aircraft was seen and it was presumed he had hit the trees and not survived the crash. He was indeed killed. Three days later was another bad day for 349. The second operation of the day proved exceptionally unlucky. Flight Lieutenant J. Mascaux crashed on take-off due to a mechanical failure. He could only remember seeing tree branches and oil or black smoke on his windscreen before he crashed on the airfield. He was taken to hospital with facial injuries but nothing too serious and the Spitfire was repaired. The rest of the formation continued, but F/Sgt J. Blair, one of the British pilots of the squadron, was shot down. When returning over Zwolle his Blue Section went down to attack a train. The flak was heavy and two minutes after making the attack he called on the R/T to say his engine temperature was high and that he would return direct to base. Three minutes later he again called saying he was okay but had force-landed and asked where he was. Blue 1 (F/L M. Mycroft - British) replied that the target was Zwolle, meaning to indicate he was in that area. His actual landing place was south-west of Zwolle. He was presumed to be unhurt and, having landed within the enemy lines, was taken prisoner soon after. A third Spitfire was also lost that day. Soon after landing on return from the third show, the Spitfire flown by F/O A. Vanderheyden caught fire; nothing could be done to save the aircraft, but the pilot was safe.

On 13 February, 349 was ordered to move to Predannack in Cornwall to convert to the Hawker Tempest. The last sorties were carried out on the 16th and a few days later the squadron was at Predannack. Conversion to the Tempest started on the 24th but that was halted a few days later when the Tempests were sent to the continent, the RAF facing a shortage of the type with 2TAF. Some

Typhoons arrived as replacements at the same time as the new CO, S/L R. Lallemant, a former Typhoon pilot with 609 Squadron who would officially take over at the end of March. The re-equipment soon proved a dead end. The squadron spent March and part of April flying Typhoons, only to be notified at the end that their return to the continent would be with Spitfires. Indeed, the squadron was re-assigned to 2TAF and placed under 132 (Norwegian) Wing authority which would provide their aircraft: Spitfire IXs! The personnel arrived at B.106/Twente, where 132 Wing was stationed, on 19 April and 349 was due to become operational on the 24th. That happened earlier as, on the 22nd, weather recces were carried out but the reports prevented any ops. The following day, however, thirty armed recces were flown even though ten aircraft returned early due to engine trouble. Operations continued on the 24th but one pilot was posted missing, F/L H. Wieck (British, on his second operational flight with the Belgians). When approximately eight miles south of Aurich, Wieck called on the R/T to say his engine was cutting out and he was about to make a forced landing. His number one turned around to search the locality but did not see him. He was eventually found safe. Luck was not on 349's side for long as, the day after, F/L A. Claessen was posted missing while attacking METs south of Wesermünde. He was last seen at treetop height making the attack. He was probably flying too low and hit the treetops and crashed. It was definitely not happy times for the Belgians as, two days later, another pilot lost his life. Flight Lieutenant J. Wood, a British pilot and the A Flight CO, was hit by flak while attacking METs near Lehmden, south of Varel. His aircraft caught fire and was seen crashing in flames. It was a deadly return to the continent for the squadron and somewhat bitter as the war's end was now so close. The following day, the 28th, 349 left 132 Wing to join 131 Wing at B.113/Varrelbush. This unit was equipped with Spitfire XVIs so the squadron finally said goodbye to its Mk.IXs.

Bad weather prevented any ops before 3 May. Various armed recces of four Spitfire XVIs were flown that day which ended with six METs, four METs famers and one staff destroyed, not counting other targets claimed as damaged. The next day, 349 sent twelve Spitfires on an armed recce of North and around Bremerhaven led by F/L Seydel. Even if four Spitfires were obliged to return early due to mechanical trouble, the rest of the formation continued the mission and were back one hour later with two more METs destroyed to 349's account and with many more claimed as damaged. That was actually the last 349's war mission and 349 flew in all 40 sorties on Spitfire XVI, ending with SM181, SM186, TB492, TB515/P, TB635, TB735/E, TB755, TB900/D, TB906/V, TB910, TD116/G, TD121, TD140/X, TD184/R, TD288, TD339 in its inventory. Then, the squadron took up the task of occupation until October 1946 when it left the RAF to become part of the re-born Belgian Air Force, the last months seeing S/L Van de Velde to be back at the squadron to command. However, between VE-Day and 24 October 1946, six major accidents were recorded, one of which causing the death of a pilot, F/Sgt M. Rémy.

349' Spitfire XVIs in Germany during the summer of 1945. *(André Bar)*

'Cheval' Lallemant was attending the *Aeronautique Militaire* Flying School when the Germans invaded Belgium in May 1940. The school was evacuated to Morocco and from there he reached England with a group of Belgian pilots in July 1940. He enlisted in the RAF and completed his training and, in September 1941, was posted to No. 609 (West Riding) Squadron as an NCO. He flew Typhoons with 609 until the end of his tour in June 1943. By that time, he was commissioned and had claimed the destruction of four Fw190s and one probable. His first claim was on 19 December 1942. He was awarded the DFC in March 1943. He then spent his rest period as a Typhoon production test pilot. He started a second tour of operations with No. 197 Squadron as a flight commander in January 1944 but his stay was brief as he was posted to No. 198 Squadron in the same role the following month. There he would make his last claims (in February) to bring his total to six confirmed victories (one shared) and one probable. In August, he returned to his initial unit to take command. His stay was short, however, as, 14 September, he was hit by ground fire, crashed and was badly burned. A Bar to his DFC was awarded in January 1945. Although not fully recovered, he returned to operations when he assumed command of No. 349 (Belgian) Squadron in March 1945, flying Spitfires this time. He led the squadron until the end of year and was released from the RAF in October 1946. He remained in the post-war Belgian Air Force and retired in 1972 as a Colonel.

Supermarine Spitfire Mk. XVI TB900
No. 349 (Belgian) Squadron
Squadron Leader R. Lallemant
B.116/Wunstorf (Germany), summer 1945

Date	Pilot	SN	Origin	Type	Serial	Code	Nb	Cat.
06.06.44	F/O Jean **Moreau de Melen**	RAF No. 138884	(bel)/RAF	Ju88	**MK178**	GE-Q	0.5	C
	F/Sgt Joseph **Moureau**	RAF No. 1299855	(bel)/RAF		**MK153**	GE-S	0.5	C
	F/Sgt Joseph **Van Molkot**	RAF No. 1814824	(bel)/RAF	Ju88	**MK363**	GE-U	0.5	C
	Sgt Jean **Bragard**	RAF No. 1424828	(bel)/RAF		**MJ955**	GE-T	0.5	C
08.06.44	F/L Gabriel **Seydel**	RAF No. 116541	(bel)/RAF	Fw190	**MK354**	GE-V	1.5	C
	W/O Douglas F. **Clarke**	NZ417018	RNZAF		**MJ955**	GE-T	0.5	C
26.07.44	F/L Gabriel **Seydel**	RAF No. 116541	(bel)/RAF	Bf109	**NH257**	GE-N	1.0	C
	F/L Paul **Siroux**	RAF No. 127853	(bel)/RAF	Bf109	**ML404**	GE-E	1.0	C
28.07.44	F/O Jean **Moreau de Melen**	RAF No. 138884	(bel)/RAF	*V-1*	**NH464**	GE-R	1.0	C

Total: 6.0 + 1 V-1

Among the Belgian pilots who scored while serving with 349 Sqn, the most successful was F/L G. Seydel (top left). He enlisted in the Belgian *Aéronautique Militaire* (AM) in September 1939 for a two-year contract and was still under training when he was evacuated with his Flying School to France then to the UK. He completed his training there and joined No. 131 Squadron in the summer of 1941 where a Belgian Flight had been raised, a flight that would become the nucleus of No. 350 (Belgian) Squadron. He completed his first tour in January 1943 and, by the end of the war, had completed another two tours with the Belgian squadrons as a flight CO. He survived the war with a DFC awarded in December 1945.

Middle, F/L P. Siroux, another flight commander, and another former NCO with the AM, was one of the few Belgians to fly the Hurricane operationally at the time. He became a PoW at the end of the campaign but was released in August 1940. He fled to the UK via Spain in October 1940 and was imprisoned for many months in Spain before being liberated and arriving in Gibraltar in January 1942. He joined the RAF and was re-trained and posted to No. 350 Squadron in January 1943, then to 349 Sqn until the end of his tour in February 1945. He survived the war and was awarded the DFC in July 1945.

F/O J. Moreau de Melen (top right) was another former pilot of the AM, an NCO newly posted to fly Fiat CR.42s when the Germans launched their offensive. He managed to avoid capture and left Belgium for the UK in November 1940, passing through Switzerland, unoccupied France and North Africa. He was arrested and spent a few months in prison before being liberated on parole in December 1941; he stayed in Morocco until the arrival of US troops in November 1942. Joining the RAF, he re-trained and joined 349 Sqn on its formation in June 1943. He served with the unit until the end of his tour in September 1944. He survived the war but held no further operational positions before the end of the war.

(André Bar)

Date	Pilot	S/N	Origin	Serial	Code	Fate
		Spitfire Mk V				
02.01.44	F/Sgt Albert Van den Broeck	RAF No. 1424850	(BEL)/RAF	BL565	GE-E	†
11.02.44	F/O Jacques Fromont	RAF No. 145065	(BEL)/RAF	AR490	GE-A	-
	P/O Jean Croquet	RAF No. 158234	(BEL)/RAF	AB175	GE-U	Eva.
		Spitfire Mk IX				
21.04.44	F/O Jean Moreau de Melen	RAF No. 138884	(BEL)/RAF	MJ962	GE-F	-
28.04.44	F/Sgt Henri Limet	RAF No. 1299911	(BEL)/RAF	MH610	GE-Z	PoW
10.05.44	F/O Paul Libert	RAF No. 161343	(BEL)/RAF	MH491		PoW
21.05.44	F/O Marcel Sans	RAF No. 138840	(BEL)/RAF	MK192	GE-H	-
28.05.44	F/O Jean Ester	RAF No. 127452	(BEL)/RAF	MK130	GE-P	-
06.06.44	F/Sgt Joseph Van Molkot	RAF No. 1814824	(BEL)/RAF	MK363	GE-U	PoW*
07.06.44	F/O Marcel Sans	RAF No. 138840	(BEL)/RAF	MJ748	GE-A	†
08.06.44	F/Sgt Jean Gheyssens	RAF No. 1814842	(BEL)/RAF	MK252	GE-F	†
12.06.44	F/Sgt René Vandenbosh	RAF No. 1814841	(BEL)/RAF	MK175	GE-B	-
04.08.44	*Destroyed on the ground by a V-1*	-	-	NH354	GE-T	-
30.08.44	F/O Maurice Renard	RAF No. 159219	(BEL)/RAF	NH199	GE-J	-
05.10.44	F/O André Vanderheyden	RAF No. 162801	(BEL)/RAF	PT730	GE-R	Eva.
06.10.44	W/O Kenneth R. Brant	RAF No. 1575979	RAF	PT395		PoW
19.10.44	F/O Camille de Saint Aubin	RAF No. 130771	(BEL)/RAF	PT841	GE-R	†
	S/L Albert Van de Velde	RAF No. 123067	(BEL)/RAF	PT555	GE-M	-
03.11.44	F/O Henri Goldsmit	RAF No. 151928	(BEL)/RAF	PT963	GE-N	†
	F/Sgt Paul Decroix	RAF No. 1424878	(BEL)/RAF	PV134		PoW
08.11.44	F/O Alexander Uydens	RAF No. 153168	(BEL)/RAF	PT891	GE-E	Inj.
19.11.44	F/O Marc Gendebien	RAF No. 153365	(BEL)/RAF	NH241		†
29.11.44	F/Sgt Raymond Van Wymers	RAF No. 1424894	(BEL)/RAF	RK838		†
25.12.44	F/O Maurice Renard	RAF No. 159219	(BEL)/RAF	RK802	GE-Q	†
01.01.45	*Destroyed in air raid*	-	-	PT830	GE-X	-
22.01.45	F/Sgt Jean Leroy	RAF No. 1424886	(BEL)/RAF	PL246	GE-M	PoW
03.02.45	F/Sgt Léon van de Werde de Vorsellaer	RAF No. 1424855	(BEL)/RAF	PT549		†
06.02.45	F/Sgt Donald Blair	RAF No. 742018	RAF	TA837	GE-S	PoW
	F/O André Vanderheyden	RAF No. 162801	(BEL)/RAF	PT946	GE-T	-
24.04.45	F/L Hubert F. Wieck	RAF No. 126983	RAF	PV185		PoW
25.04.45	F/L Antoon Claesen	RAF No. 125846	(BEL)/RAF	NH488	GE-W	†
27.04.45	F/L John Wood	RAF No. 139514	RAF	MK830	GE-X	†

Total: 32

*Liberated by US troops in August

Eight Belgian pilots of A Flight: (L-R) P/O M. Siraut, F/O M. Balasse (†23.01.45 with 41 Sqn), F/Sgt L. Verbeeck, F/O J. Moreau de Melen; P/O A. Moureau, P/O H. Bailly, Sgt C. Brahy and Sgt J. Groensteen (†20.04.45).
Flying Officer Balasse left 349 in November 1943 for 41 Sqn where he became a V1 ace while flying Spitfire XIIs. *(André Bar)*

In front of dispersal: (L-R) F/Sgt A. Van den Broek († 02.01.44), Sgt G. Halleux, F/O J. Moreau de Melen, Sgt J. Groensteen (†20.04.45), F/O A. Lemaire, F/Sgt L. Verbeeck, F/O A. Van Hecke (†12.10.43), F/L H. Gulson (Adjutant, British), P/O A. Moureau.
(André Bar)

Some Belgian pilots posing with one of the squadron's first Spitfire IXs, complete with the squadron emblem that would be used for the future squadron crest. This emblem was short-lived and had disappeared by D-Day.
Above, on the wing: Flying Officers M. Siraut (who designed the emblem) and J. Ester.
On top: F/Sgt J. Van Molkot, Flying Officers A. Lemaire and J. Moreau de Melen, F/Sgt R. Vandenbosch, and P/O H. Goldsmit (†03.11.44). In the cockpit is F/Sgt H. Limet. All but Goldsmit were veterans of the May 1940 campaign with the Belgian Army or the Belgian *Aéronautique Militaire*.
Below, the same group of pilots now posing aside 349's emblem: Standing: F/O M. Siraut, P/O H. Goldsmit, Flying Officers A. Lemaire, J. Moreau de Melen and J. Ester, and F/Sgt J. Van Molkot and, on top, F/Sgt R. Vandenbosch with F/Sgt H. Limet still in the cockpit.
(André Bar)

On readiness, left to right: F/Sgt J. Gheyssens (†08.06.44), Flying Officers J. Fromont, P. Libert (a former NCO pilot wounded on 10 May 1940 during the bombardment of Schaffen airfield), H. Taymans (†28.11.44), and H. Goldsmit (†03.11.44), P/O H. Bailly (a former Fairey Fox pilot shot down on 15 May 1940), F/L J. Morai, P/O G. Halleux, F/O J. Ester (previously with No. 350 Squadron, shot down on 16 June 1942, imprisoned by the French, then the Italians, before being liberated on parole in April 1943), F/L G. Seydel, and Flight Sergeants H. Limet and J. Moureau. *(André Bar)*

Below, some pilots during the winter of 1944-1945.
Front, left to right: Sgt J-P. Lacoste, F/O J. Croquet, S/L A. Van de Velde (the CO), and F/L A. Claesen (†25.04.45). Claesen was an experienced pilot who had previously served with Nos. 350 and 232 Squadrons. When he joined 349 Sqn in January 1945, it was his second tour. Top: Flight Sergeants H. Branders and D. Blair (British, PoW 06.02.45), W/O D. A. Smerdon (British), F/L J. Wood (British, †27.04.45), F/Sgt L. van de Werve (†03.02.45), and F/O L. Paulis (IO).

Date	Pilot	S/N	Origin	Serial	Code	Fate
	KITTYHAWK Mk II					
09.04.43	F/Sgt Ernest **ORBRART**	RAF No. 1380519	RAF	**FS401**	349 Sqn	†
	SPITFIRE Mk V					
25.07.43	P/O Maurice **BALASSE**	RAF No. 135893	(BEL)/RAF	**BL389**		-
12.10.43	P/O Albrecht **VAN HECKE**	RAF No. 135895	(BEL)/RAF	**AD292**		†
31.01.44	F/Sgt Henri **LIMET**	RAF No. 1299911	(BEL)/RAF	**AB870**		-
12.02.44	F/L Albert **VAN DE VELDE**	RAF No. 123067	(BEL)/RAF	**EP354**	GE-L	-
	Ground collision with EP354	-	-	**AR432**	GE-G	-
	SPITFIRE Mk IX					
15.04.44	F/Sgt René **VANDENBOSH**	RAF No. 1814841	(BEL)/RAF	**MK136**	GE-N	-
29.04.44	F/Sgt Alfred **MOUREAU**	RAF No. 1299851	(BEL)/RAF	**MJ296**	GE-C	-
12.07.44	F/O Arthur A.G. **PATINY**	RAF No. 153064	RAF	**NH464**		†
	SPITFIRE Mk XVI					
15.09.45	F/Sgt Jean-Pierre **LACOSTE**	RAF No. 1424998	(BEL)/RAF	**TB355**	GE-V	-
20.09.45	Sgt David **DE MERVIUS**	RAF No. 1814839	(BEL)/RAF	**TD116**	GE-G	-
17.12.45	F/Sgt Maurice **RÉMY**	RAF No. 1424995	(BEL)/RAF	**TD232**	GE-A	†
13.02.46	P/O Gustave **DELBECQ**	RAF No. 201883	(BEL)/RAF	**TD121**		-
21.03.46	W/O Fernand **DE DEKEN**	RAF No. 1299859	(BEL)/RAF	**RK243**		-
19.06.46	F/Sgt Hubert **HOYBERGEN**	RAF No. 797773	(BEL)/RAF	**TB910**	GE-J	-

Total: 15

On 5 October 1943, Spitfire V AA994/GE-U sustained slight damage through running into a pile of earth towards the end of the runway. The trouble was caused through the failure of the pneumatic
system which affected the flaps and brakes. The pilot Sgt J. Moreau was uninjured. *(André Bar)*

A line-up of 349's Spitfire Mk.Vs in January 1944 with AA751/GE-K, AR490/GE-A, AD295/GE-P and BL642/GE-C visible. Below, close-up on AR490/GE-A
(André Bar)

Spitfire XVI TB991/GE-L in flight over Germany.
Below, Spitfire XVI TB735/GE-E at Wunstorf.
(André Bar)

Squadron Leader Lallemant's Spitfire XVI TB900/GE-D seen with two markings variations.
(André Bar)

Before the transfer to the Belgian Air Force of the two Belgian squadrons, they were authorised to wear the Belgian roundels. Above TB991/GE-L and below GE-J.
(André Bar)

Daniel Le Roy du Vivier
RAF No. 82159

Daniel Le Roy du Vivier was an NCO pilot with the Belgian *Aéronautique Militaire* flying Fairey Fireflies when the Germans launched their offensive on Belgium and the Low Countries on 10 May 1940. He moved to France with his unit a couple of days later and on 19 June he left for the United Kingdom. Arriving in early July, he joined No. 43 Squadron in August 1940 as a Pilot Officer, after a short refresher course at No. 7 OTU, and claimed his first victory on 16 August against a Ju87 (plus another damaged). Wounded in combat on 2 September, he recovered to be posted to No. 229 Squadron where he made further claims (two probables, one shared) before returning to No. 43 Squadron to become a flight commander in April. More successes were recorded the following month. On 15 January 1942 he was finally appointed OC of the squadron thus becoming the first non-British Commonwealth pilot to command an RAF unit. He had been awarded the DFC a couple of days previously. On 28 May he claimed a Ju88 destroyed, his last claim, to bring his total to five confirmed victories (two shared), two probably destroyed (one shared) and one damaged. In September 1942 he relinquished command and a Bar to his DFC was added two months later. After various non-operational postings he was sent to the Middle East in April 1943 and posted to an HQ position. In June he went to No. 239 Wing as supernumerary Wing Commander to gain experience as a Wing Leader, but had a ground accident on 31 July that kept him away from flying for several months. In January 1944, he was authorised to return to operations and after a couple of weeks at No. 239 Wing, he became Wing Leader of No. 324 Wing in March 1944. This was his last operational posting before the end of the war. He returned to the UK in July 1944 and became the OC of No. 53 OTU the following month, a position he held until May 1945. In April 1946 he took command of No. 160 (Belgian) Wing in Germany before leaving the service in September.

Supermarine Spitfire Mk. XVI TB590
No. 160 (Belgian) Wing
Wing Commander D. Le Roy du Vivier
B.152/Fassberg (Germany), summer 1946

To administer Nos. 349 and 350 Squadrons, No. 160 (Belgian) Wing was formed at Fassberg in Germany in August 1945 whose commander in the summer of 1946 was Wing Commander D. Le Roy du Viver. The entire wing was transferred to the Belgian Air Force on 25 October 1946 to become No. 1 Wing at Beauvechain.
(André Bar)

SQUADRONS! - The series

Donald James Matthew BLAKESLEE DFC

Supermarine Spitfire Mk.VB EN951
No. 133 (Eagle) Squadron
Flight Lieutenant D. J. M. Blakeslee
CAN./ J.4551
Gravesend (UK), August 1942

Charles Cuthbertson LEARMONTH DFC*

(Douglas Boston Mk. III A28-6 (ex-AL891))
No. 22 Squadron RAAF
Squadron Leader C. C. Learmonth
Port Moresby (New Guinea), spring 1943

Hans Anton MAURENBRECHER

Curtiss P-40N-35-CU C3-560
No. 120 (NEI) Squadron
Major H. Maurenbrecher
Biak (New Guinea), 1943-1946

Roland Prosper BEAMONT DSO* DFC*

Hawker Tempest Mk.V JN751
No. 150 Wing
Wing Commander R. P. Beamont
RAF No. 91820
Bradwell Bay (UK), April 1944

Ronald Thomas SUSANS DSO DFC

North American P-51D-25-NT A68-724
No. 77 Squadron, RAAF
Squadron Leader R. T. Susans
O4590
Iwakuni (Japan), 1947

James Henry LACEY DFM

Supermarine Spitfire Mk.XIV RN135
No. 17 Squadron
Squadron Leader J. H. Lacey
RAF No. 112798
Seletar (Singapore), autumn 1945

Introducing's RAF In Combat and Bravo Bravo Aviation's collection of highly-detailed and historically accurate, high-quality aviation prints.
For more information on available prints, please visit :

www.RAF-IN-COMBAT.com   or

BRAVO BRAVO AVIATION
BBA
HIGH QUALITY AVIATION ILLUSTRATION
www.BravoBravoAviation.com

Yvan du MONCEAU de BERGENDAEL DFC*

Supermarine Spitfire Mk.IX MJ-365
No. 349 (Belgian) Squadron
Squadron Leader Y. du Monceau de Bergendael
RAF No. 87700
Selsey (UK), June 1944

Daniel LE ROY DU VIVIER DFC*

Supermarine Spitfire Mk. XVI TB590
No. 160 (Belgian) Wing
Wing Commander D. Le Roy du Vivier
RAF No. 82159
B.152/Fassberg (Germany), summer 1946

Prints available for this book:

PL-013: Y. du Monceau (1)
PL-014: Y. du Monceau (2)
PL-018: A. Guillaume
PL-026: M. Donnet
PL-058: A. Boussa (1)
PL-061: A. Boussa (2)
PL-062: T. Spencer
PL-086: J.M. Thompson
PL-120: D. Le Roy du Vivier
PL-121: H.E. Walmsley
PL-122: A. Plisnier
PL-123: F. Venesoen
PL-124: R. Lallemant
PL-125: A. Van de Velde
PL-126: L. Collignon